D1859840

VADAVALI OF JAYATRITHA
SANSKRIT-ENGLISH

Owing to the antiquity and rarity of this book, certain pages are regrettably absent, and readability is compromised due to the blurring of the original text. If you possess any insights regarding the availability of these missing sections, kindly inform us. Your assistance is crucial in ensuring the completion of this significant work for the benefit of future generations.

VADAVALI OF JAYATRITHA SANSKRIT-ENGLISH

JAYATRITHA

Published by

Isha Books
B-63, Ist Floor
New Gupta Colony
Near DDA Market
Delhi - 110009

Distribution Network
gyanbooks.com
India, USA, Canada, UK, Australia

© Publisher
All rights reserved. No part of this work may be reproduced, stored, adapted, or transmitted in any form or by any means, electronic, mechanical, photocopying, micro-filming, recording or otherwise, or translated in any language, without the prior written permission of the copyright owner and the publisher.

ISBN: 978-93-3317-438-1 (HB)
First Published, 1943

2nd Impression 2025

Printed at: Gyan Press, Delhi.

The book is sold subject to the condition that it shall not, by way of trade or otherwise, be lent, resold, hired out, or otherwise circulated without the prior publisher's written consent.

VADAVALI OF JAYATRITHA SANSKRIT-ENGLISH
Author: JAYATRITHA

VĀDĀVALĪ

BY

JAYATĪRTHA

EDITED WITH AN ENGLISH TRANSLATION

BY

P. NAGARAJA RAO, M.A.

Department of Philosophy, Benares Hindu University

THE ADYAR LIBRARY, ADYAR

1943

The Adyar Library Series No. 40

GENERAL EDITOR:
G. SRINIVASA MURTI, B.A., B.L., M.B. & C.M., VAIDYARATNA
Director, Adyar Library

VĀDĀVALĪ BY JAYATIRTHA

a criticism from Dvaita stand-point of the doctrine of the illusoriness of the universe

(MITHYĀTVA-KHANDANA)

DEDICATED TO
My Father and Mother
with love, veneration and gratitude

FOREWORD

THIS is the first time that the Adyar Library has published a work bearing on the Dvaita School of Vedānta. It is our desire to publish in our series standard works dealing with the different aspects of Indian thought, namely, religion, philosophy, literature, arts etc. No apology is needed in having selected the Vādāvalī of Jayatīrtha as the first work in our series bearing on the Dvaita School. It is admitted by all that Jayatīrtha is the greatest exponent of Madhva's philosophy and this work tackles the most important problem on which the Advaitins and the Dvaitins differ fundamentally, namely, the reality or the illusoriness of difference in the Universe.

The edition of the work was prepared by Mr. P. Nagaraja Rao, now a member of the Department of Philosophy in the Benares Hindu University. The edition with an English translation and notes was undertaken by him when he was a Research Fellow in the Department of Indian Philosophy in the University of Madras; the late Mr. S. S. Suryanarayana Sastri, the Head of the Department supervised his work. With the permission of the University, the publication of the work was entrusted to the Adyar Library in the second half of 1942.

About the time the Library was able to start printing, Mr. Suryanarayana Sastri passed away suddenly after a brief illness. This very tragic event further delayed the starting of printing and it could be taken up only in February 1943. It is a great loss that Mr. Suryanarayana Sastri himself could not supervise the printing of the book. The editor, Mr. Nagaraja Rao is also far away in Benares. Thus the work of passing the proofs had to be undertaken by myself. I revised the manuscript of the translation and I took the liberty of introducing many alterations. I am also responsible for dividing the text into a large number of small sections. For any defect found in the book, a good share must fall on my own shoulders. The notes are printed practically in the form in which the manuscripts were placed in my hands ; I have made only few corrections and these only when I was satisfied that they were scribal errors.

The translation is divided in this edition into a large number of main sections. The notes form a sort of running commentary on the translation and each note refers to the whole of such a section. Each such division deals with a particular main topic. The division into smaller sections is introduced to facilitate the comparison of the text with the translation. Further it gives an analytical view of the subject.

In preparing the edition, we have followed mainly the text published from Kumbakonam. The Belgaum edition too has been consulted. At the end of each main section, the Kumbakonam edition gives the subject of that section. But in this edition the text is printed continuously without indicating such divisions. The main division noted in the translation has been introduced only for the sake of the notes. The points dealt with in the main divisions are given in the contents, both in Sanskrit and in English.

The additional notes at the end deal with certain specific points in the text, as distinct from the running commentary included in the main notes. They were first given as foot-notes. But I transferred them to the end since I felt that foot-notes coming after the text and the translation at the bottom of the page may affect the general appearance of the printed pages. Since the text and the translation have been divided into very small sections there will be no difficulty in identifying the passage to which these additional notes refer.

I prepared the index at the end of the book. It contains nearly all important words in the text. For nouns, I have not grouped the words separately for different declensional forms. But the verbs are given in their full grammatical form. Sometimes in compound words, only some members are given. It is hoped that this index will enable the readers to find out a section very easily. It will also be of help to find out the translation of a particular word or techinical term.

This volume in the Adyar Library Series will be a companion volume to the edition of the Vedāntaparibhāṣā recently issued from the Library as No. 34.

A comprehensive exposition of the Viśiṣṭādvaita Philosophy by Prof. P. N. Srinivasachari is also expected to be issued very soon from the Library. The Vādāvalī does not deal with all the topics found in the Vedāntaparibhāṣā; perhaps Jayatīrtha's Pramāṇapaddhati would have been a better and more appropriate choice as a companion volume to the Vedāntaparibhāṣā. As a matter of fact, this work of Jayatīrtha may also find a place in the Library Series at an early date, as soon as the present scarcity of paper is removed and printing becomes a practicable problem again. Vādāvalī is more a refutation of the Advaita doctrine than a presentation of the Dvaita view; yet on this particular point, we cannot think of a better work.

In the translation, the editor has paid as much attention to the accuracy of the rendering as to the readability of the Engligh version. English language has yet to settle down to its form in conveying Sanskritic ideas. A translator has to confine himself to the available vocabulary of English to express the ideas found in the Sanskrit original; English words have acquired a significance which will not always be indentical with the strict sense of the Sanskrit word. Until by convention and usage the words and the modes of expression in the English language fashion themselves properly for this new purpose, critics can always find fault with the translation by pointing out the unsuitability of a particular word or of a particular way of constructing a sentence. The word Brahman is retained in English without attempting to find out a corresponding English word, if there is one. But in the case of words like pramāṇa (means of valid knowledge) and ātman (self) the English words are selected, though the words are fairly well known to those who are familiar with Indian thought. Ākāśa is another difficult word, which is translated as ether. But in many places, as in sections 220, 309, 310 etc. (where the word used is *nabhas*), it means the sky-vault and in other places it means mere space as in sections 344 and 424. Sometimes the words in Sanskrit, if mechanically rendered into English will carry no sense without other words; in such cases the additional words are given in brackets. Again a word may be clear in Sanskrit; but it will not be quite explicit in the English version. In such cases, some explanation or the antecedent of a pronoun is given in brackets. It is true that such modes result in a sort of unevenness in the English passages; but at the present stage in the English translation of Sanskrit works of a very technical nature, intelligibility and accuracy must have preference over elegance of style.

Jayatīrtha's style is very terse, to the point, and full of meaning. His analysis is thorough; he hits hard. These are qualities which cannot be faithfully carried over into the translation also. One misses much when one passes from the Sanskrit original to the English version. But I must congratulate the translator in having preserved so much of the force of the original in the translation. The fact that the late

Mr. Suryanarayana Sastri had supervised the translation is sufficient guarantee for the value and accuracy of the translation. Perhaps he would have improved the present version if he had seen the proofs in the course of printing.

About Jayatīrtha and his place in the Dvaita Vedānta and also in Indian philosophical literature, the translator has given a brief account in the introduction. His style is at the same time terse and lucid. His analysis of the various intricate points is very minute and at the same time it is very clear. The language is elegant and at the same time very forceful. For unassailable logic there are few works that can be a match to this work of Jayatīrtha.

As for the doctrines, it is better that lesser people like me do not express an opinion where the great Ācāryas differ. To understand the position take up by S'aṅkara regarding the illusory nature (mitthyātva) of the world that we experience, one has to look at the Buddhistic position. The Buddhists rely on dry logic and attempt to prove that everything positive is momentary and unreal and that s'ūnya (void) is the only reality. S'aṅkara takes up their very logic to prove that our mind is incapable of cognising a negative aspect. This negation may be in point of space, in point of time or in point of the different things themselves. S'aṅkara shows that every such negation, *i.e.*, difference, is indeterminable (anirvacanīya). Difference is an object of experience and as such it is not absolutely unreal and since it is sublated on the realisation of Truth, it is not absolutely real also. We determine things as either what is or what is not. Difference is neither. In this way it is indeterminable. The problem is whether difference is sublated at the time of the realisation of the Truth. Vedic passages simply state what that Truth is. The interpretation of such passages depend on the realisation of Truth. Thus intil Truth is realised, one cannot say whether difference is sublated at all. If it is not sublated, it is absolutely real. In the Advaita system, sublatability is not the factor which militates against the absolute reality of difference. The writers on Advaita attempt to show that the congition of difference is a psychological impossibility. Such a cognition, according to them cannot result in a valid knowledge, because cognition of one difference depends on the cognition of another difference and this latter depends on the former. Thus there cannot be a really valid cognition of difference. The great contribution of S'aṅkara is in establishing the positive nature of the world as against the nihilistic view of the Buddhists, taking his stand on the very platform of the Buddhists, namely, pure logic. Buddhists defined everything in terms of difference; difference from other things is the real nature of a thing, according to the Buddhists. This is what is called the apohavāda. S'aṅkara shows that the pure positive existence is the only real factor in a thing.

But the doctrine of S'aṅkara did not continue in its purity. The emphasis was slightly shifted. The illusory nature of the world and not the illusory nature of difference in the world became the chief point in Advaita. But to S'aṅkara, the world freed from difference is the reality. Thus what was originally a doctrine of the absolutely positive nature of the Universe came to be presented as a doctrine of the illusory nature of the Universe. The Dvaita school attempted to re-establish the real nature of the Universe. The difference between S'aṅkara and Madhva is not on the problem of "realism". S'aṅkara was as much a realist as Madhva. The main contention was on the problem of differences in this real world. S'aṅkara was a pure realist without accepting the possibility of any kind of negation as a reality in this Universe. To Madhva, realism is conditioned by possibilities of negation in point of time, space and mutual indentity, as real factors in the Universe. When we start a theory of antethesis between the two great Ācāryas, we must also recognise the limitations of such an entethesis.

It is my great privilege to introduce this first publication of the Adyar Library of a work dealing with Dvaita philosophy, not as a rival of the Vedāntaparibhāṣa recently published, but as presenting another view regarding the nature of the Universe. Thus the two go as companion volumes and not as opponents in the field of Indian philosophy. I take this opportunity to express my sense of gratitude to the late Mr. Suryanarayana Sastri for all that he has done to the students of Philosophy and to the Adyar Library in particular, through his contributions and I take the liberty to dedicate my part in this work to his sacred memory. Mr. P. Nagaraja

Rao deserve the sincere thanks of the Adyar Library for bringing out such an excellent translation with notes of one of the most important works in Dvaita philosophy. I thank the Madras University for giving the necessary permission for issuing this book in the Adyar Library series. This book was printed in just two months and the entire credit goes to the Vasanta Press. If there are any printing mistakes, the responsibility is entirely on me. I must specially thank the Manager of the Vasanta Press for the promptness with which the printing was executed, especially when the speed has not in any way prejudiced the interests of get up and general appearance.

As I was closely associated with the late Mr. Suryanarayana Sastri in various literary activities for fifteen years, I consider it a great privilege to have had this opportunity of seeing through the press this volume which was prepared under his supervision. I must confess that when I was passing the proof, I missed my colleague very much. Whenever I had difficulties in the matter of the translation of any particular passage, I took the liberty to make the necessary revision, with the full confidence that he was closely watching my work from above and was ever guiding me in the difficult work entrusted to me. If he were alive, he would have written this Foreword and I have undertaken the task as his colleague in the University of Madras and as his close companion in academic activities for a long time.

In closing this Foreword I shall be failing in my duty if I do not make it clear that this work would not have been published in such a short time but for the great interest which Dr. G. Srinivasa Murti, the Director of the Adyar Library took in the general affairs of the Library and in this book in particular. It has all along been his great desire to include a standard work on Dvaita philosophy in the Adyar Library Series; when I suggested the publication of this book, he readily agreed to it. In spite of financial difficulties and scarcity of paper, he promptly gave precedence to this work over some others that had already been started or had been accepted for publication. I record my very hearty thanks to him.

Adyar Library C. KUNHAN RAJA
29th April, 1943

ANALYTICAL TABLE OF CONTENTS

PAGE

विषयसङ्ग्रहः

CORRECTIONS

१४. ध्रुवः

१६. तन्नात्मत्वप्रयुक्तं

५४. प्रथमोत्पन्नप्रदीपप्रभावत्

११६. प्रमाणागम्यत्वेन

१७९. चात्मा ज्ञानस्याकार

२०६. त्रिकालासत्यता

२३२. प्रमाणविषयतानभ्युपगमाच्च

२३७. अत्यन्तासत्त्वाभ्युपगन्तृवादिन

२३८. प्रमाणदृष्टत्वात्

२७१. किमात्मनोऽन्यः ?

२७२. चोपलभ्येरन्

२७३. विनष्टा

२७५. करणेनोपलभ्यन्ते

२९४. उत्तरोत्तरप्रपञ्चारोपे

३२१. संसर्गनिरूपणाद्विति

३७९. between the attributes (in substrates that are not different).

४२४. झटिति

४३०. गन्ध इति

४९८. निगडादिदृष्टान्तस्य

५०६. अन्तःकरणादेः

५१३. अभयमेव च

INTRODUCTION

S'RĪ MADHVA'S Dvaita Vedānta is the most powerful reaction against the non-dualism of S'rī S'aṅkara. It is a pluralistic system of metaphysics based on the most radically realistic epistemology with a perfect grounding in devout theism. Times without number, in the course of his commentaries and independent tracts S'rī Madhva maintained that the chief mission of his life was to refute the claim of the Advaitin that his system had the sanction and support of the scriptures, and to demonstrate the fact of the inerrancy of his own interpretation of scriptures, on the ground that he was the chosen prophet of Lord Viṣṇu commissioned to interpret the vedas aright and vindicate " the ways of God to man ". This task Madhva sought to achieve through all his thirty-seven works. Almost all his works are very terse and they make no meaning without the illuminating commentary of Jayatīrtha.

Jayatīrtha (1365—1388) is the greatest among the disciples of Madhva.[1] He has commented on almost all the important works of Madhva. Tradition holds the view that the mission of his life was to reveal the *gurubhāva* (the thoughts of the Master). He is called the *ṭīkācārya* (the commentator *par excellence*) and not the author of *ṭippaṇis*

[1] *Age of Jayatīrtha* by B. N. Krishnamurthy Sarma, *New Indian Antiquary*, Vol. I, No. 7.

(minor glosses). But for the commentaries of Jayatīrtha, Dvaita Vedānta might not have attained the status of a philosophical system. There are two accounts of his life, the *Aṇujayatīrthavijaya* and *Bṛhadjayatīrtha-vijaya*. Both of them are from the pen of Vyāsarāya. There are no historical inscriptions or other documents relating to him. He was the son of a Mahārāṣṭra Brahmin of an officer's rank, by name Raghunāth Des'pāṇḍe, and his wife Rukmābai. They lived in a village named Mangaḷveḍhe about 12 miles south-east of Pandharpur. Jayatīrtha prior to his saṁnyāsa was called Dhoṇḍo Pant Raghunāth. As a boy he was a sturdy athelete and was in the habit of riding. Early in life he was married to two wives. In his twentieth year on a summer noon, after an active hunting expedition he went to quench his thirst to the banks of the river *Candrabhāgā*, and there bending down his head from on horse-back he drank water. On the other side of the river there was the famous sage Akṣobhyatīrtha who was drawn towards the rider drinking water in a strange manner. After a short interview with the Des'pāṇde, Akṣobhya was able to give spiritual insight to him. He soon took orders under the name of Jayatīrtha.

Over twenty two works are attributed to him and most of them are printed. Among the commentaries, his *Nyāya-sudhā* takes the first place. It is an immortal work exhibiting the several facets of Jayàtīrtha's genius and his ability as a dialectician. Though his works are designated by the unassuming name of " commentary ", in reality they are first rate classics. Judged by the brilliance of his style, and his logical acumen he ranks with the great makers of philosophical style, S'abara, S'aṅkara and Vācaspati. As a dialectician he is ready for action, ready to deal blows on all sides ; sometimes he carries the attack into the enemy's camp and at other times he retreats into a defensive position. All on a sudden he steps into the arena with a new offensive. He has complete command and mastery of all the weapons for a philosophical disputation. He makes a free use of the *vitaṇḍā* type of argument, and he has for it the sanction of Madhva.

He has, to his credit, two independent works *Pramāṇa-Paddhati* and *Vādāvalī*. The first is the epistemological manual of Dvaita Vedānta. In it he examines the problems of theory of knowledge. The *Vādāvalī* is a polemical tract that criticises the Advaitin's doctrine of Māyā. It is in about seven hundred *granthas*. It is also called *Vādamālā*. The arguments of this book summarise the four Prakaraṇas of S'rī Madhva, namely *Upādhikhaṇḍana*, *Māyāvādakhaṇḍana*, *Prapañcamithyātvānumānakhaṇḍana* and *Tattvodyota*[1]. This is the earliest polemical tract of the post-Madhva period and it is the mūla for the famous *Nyāyāmṛta* of Vyāsarāya.

The Central theme of *Vādāvalī* is the refutation of the illusory nature of the universe maintained by the Advaitin. This is essential to the establishment of Dvaita Vedānta. The ultimate reality of the universe is a fundamental and necessary tenet in the establishment of the supermacy of Lord Viṣṇu, the abode of infinite auspicious attributes. He is referred to in the *Vedānta Sūtra* (Chap. I, Pāda 1, Sūtra 2) as the creator, sustainer, etc. of this universe. And if this universe, His creation, turns out to be an illusory one, it militates against His omnipotence. If the universe is illusory its creator turns out to be no better than a juggler in rags who goes out giving performances in magic to eke out his livelihood. Such a Lord cannot be the giver of mokṣa, nor can he be an object of meditation. Madhva is keen on establishing the reality of the

[1] Dr. R. Nagaraja Sarma's *Reign of Realism* gives a running exposition of the ten prakaraṇas of Madhva in English

universe in order to avoid the above mentioned contingencies in respect of the Lord.

The central doctrine of Advaita is the illusory nature of this universe. The term "mithyā" means illusion characterised as indeterminable either as real or as unreal. The whole of Advaita dialectics rests on two general postulates: (1) the absolutely real is never sublated and (2) the absolutely unreal is never cognised. The examples for the absolutely real is Brahman and that for the absolutely unreal is the horns of a hare. In between these two categories the world of plurality is caught. For the world of plurality there is the temporary sublation in deep sleep; hence it is not real. The world of plurality is cognised, hence it is not unreal. It cannot be real and unreal at the same time because it violates the law of contradiction. It is this indeterminable nature of the universe in terms of the real and the unreal that is connoted by the term "Māyā." It is not non-existence. It has practical efficiency, why, it alone has practical efficiency. Māyā has for its jurisdiction everything excepting Brahman and absolute non-existence.

The doctrine of Māyā has been subjected to a great deal of criticism by the realist. *Vādāvalī* is one such attempt. Post-S'aṅkara Advaita dialecticians have attempted to establish the illusory nature of the universe through the employment of various pramāṇas like perception, inference, scripture, experience etc. The author of the *Vādāvalī* states the Advaitin's pramāṇas in respect of the establishment of the illusory nature of the universe and refutes them in detail. The first half of the book is a criticism of the three famous inferences of the Advaitin to establish the illusory nature of the universe. The inferences have three distinct probans, namely cognisability, inertness, and finitude and the probandum with the subject is "the world under dispute is illusory." The example is the famous shell-silver. The criticism of this inference is from the point of view of formal logic. There is a statement of Madhva to the effect that all the fallacies relating to inference are found in the "three inferences" adduced by the Advaitin to establish the illusory nature of the universe.

The proposition, "the world under dispute is illusory" is taken up for criticism. The probandum "mithyātva" is resolved to mean seven alternatives, (1) indeterminability, (2) unreality, (3) being different from the real, (4) being the content of valid cognition, (5) being the content of invalid cognition, (6) being nescience or a product thereof and, (7) being cognised in the same locus as its own absolute non-existence. Each of these alternatives is examined in detail and all of them are found to contradict the canons of logic.

It is argued that there is no middle ground between reality and unreality and hence the defect, "non-establishment of the probandum" *viz., indeterminability.* It is urged that it is contradictory to hold the view that mithyāvata is "to be different from the real and unreal", because it is contradictory to hold such a view. The first alternative, "indeterminability" and the sixth alternative "nescience or its product thereof," are discussed in great detail. The concept of indeterminability is attempted to be established with the help of some inferences, and they are pointed out to be defect-ridden. Besides, counter-inferences are set forth to bring out the parity in respect of the fallaciousness. The two postulates of Advaita *i.e.*, "that which is real is not sublated", and "that which is unreal is not cognised" are criticised in detail by resolving the term real to mean one of four alternatives. In a similar manner the second postulate is also criticised.

The sixth alternative, "nescience", is discussed in eighteen sections. The term "nescience" is resolved to mean one of three things: (1) what is beginningless and interminable, (2) that which, while being a beginningless existent, is destructible by cognition and (3) the material cause of delusion. And each of these alternatives is criticised. Along with some other inferences, the famous *Vivaraṇa* inference for the establishment of the positive nature of nescience (bhāva-rūpa-avidyā) is taken up for detailed criticism and its relative parts are examined and refuted. Counter-inferences are set forth. Then the arguments from sleep-experience (sauṣuptika-anubhava), etc., for the establishment of the positive nature of nescience are refuted. Towards the end of this topic *i.e.*, the criticism of the "probandum", the author of *Vādāvalī* maintains that the Dvaitins admission of a positive nature of nescience does not militate against his criticism of the Advaitin's position, because the nescience for the Dvaitin is real (svabhāva) and it is not a super-imposition. Besides, any definition adduced in respect of nescience is acceptable to the Dvaitin. From section 134 there is the criticism of the three probans, "cognisability", "inertness" and "finitude", in detail. Each of these terms is resolved into alternatives and refuted. In the course of the criticism of "cognisability", the discussion of the Advaitin's doctrine of "Self-luminosity" (svaprakāśatvam) is taken up and unintelligibility is attributed to it. The great Advaita teacher Citsukha's definition of self-luminosity is taken up for a detailed criticism.

After the criticism of the probans, sublation by perception is urged in respect of the Advaitin's inference. Perceptions like the "pot is real" sublate the inference of the Advaitin. The relative importance of the two Pramāṇas, perception and inference, is discussed and the superior and the primary validity of perception over inference is sought to be established. In this connection, the author makes a significant remark. " If it be contended that inference itself be the sublator of perception, when perception is not sublated by another perception of equal strength, what then alas! is the talk of the wretch inference which lives at the feet of perception being the sublator of that ? "

The conflict of the Advaitin's inference with scriptural statements like " the world is real . . .", etc., is stated. In this connection the Advaitin's contention *i.e.*, that the scriptural statements which have for their import the reality of the universe are restated in order to be refuted by other scriptural statements that refute the reality of the universe, is dismissed as being untenable. Further, the Dvaitin contends that there is no need for restating a view that is not valid merely for the sake of denunciation. Besides, the conflict with the scriptural statements and the conflict with the statements of smṛtis are also pointed out.

Contradiction of the Advaitin's inferences by other inferences such as " the world under disputes is real, because it is validly cognised like Brahman etc." is pointed out. The adjunct *doṣagamyatvam* is urged as vitiating the inference of the Advaitin. The example in the Advaitin's inference, ' shell-silver ', is urged to be devoid of the *probandum*, mithyātva. There is an interesting discussion about the epistemological status of the shell-silver cognition. A counter-inference (tarka) is urged against the Advaitin's inference resulting in the acceptance of two real worlds (section 266 ff.). The validity and the tenability of the counter-inference in rebutting the Advaitin's inference, is discussed at some length.

From section 295, another famous inference of the Advaitin is taken up for criticism. It is called the " aṁśitva anumāna ".

'Being a whole' is the *probans* of the famous inference. It is criticised and refuted by pointing out defects like sublation, establishment of the established, etc. After this, it is pointed out that the *probans* of the Advaitin has no probative value, because it is of no service in the establishment of the probandum. Some of the famous srutis cited by the Advaitins in their favour such as "Neha nānāsti", "ekamevādvitīyam" etc. are criticised and they are interpreted as not going against the reality of the universe.

So far, the Dvaitin established the reality of the universe as against the contention that it is illusory. He now proceeds to establish the reality of the *five-fold differences* that are eternal. They are: (1) the difference between the Lord and soul, (2) between the Lord and Matter, (3) between soul and soul, (4) between soul and matter and, (5) between matter and matter. So, before establishing all these differences at once, he takes up the criticism of the Advaita position, "that the souls are not ultimately different from Brahman." The Advaita argument is set forth in the form of an inference, and is refuted by the Dvaitin. Similar inferences of the Advaitin attempting to establish the illusory nature of difference are refuted at great length. The various pramāṇas that are adduced for the establishment of the illusory nature of difference such as perception, inference, etc. are refuted in great detail. As a pluralist Jayatīrtha feels the need to establish the intelligibility of the concept of difference as against the Advaita dialectics arrayed against it. All the arguments of the monist to demostrate the obstacles in the way of a really valid definition of the concept of difference are set forth in extenso and refuted. From section 312 to the end of the book, the chief topic is the dialectics of difference. Difference according to S'rī Madhava is not cognised by itself but only in relation to its terms. It is not an attribute of both the relata; it is an attribute of one and it is signalised by the other. Difference is not an attribute different from the substrate. It is the svarūpa of the substrate itself. All the objections against treating difference as the svarūpa of the Dharmin (substrate) are answered at great length. Though difference is said to be of the very nature of the substrate, it is distinguishable by the assumption of the category vis'eṣa. The category vis'eṣa helps us to distinguish such of those attributes from the substrate, that are non-different from the substrate. Vis'eṣa is self-differentiating. It needs no external help. This category is discussed briefly in this connection. The witness-consciousness is responsible for the simultaneous cognition of the substrate and its attribute, difference, which is of its very nature. A discussion about the capacities of Sakṣin and his power to apprehend the validity in cogntion, Time, Ākās'a, etc. is taken up closely. A few section are devoted te the establishment of the intrinsic nature of validity and the extrinsic nature of invalidity. Rival views are sought to be refuted. The book ends with two counter-inferences pillorying the Advaitin's doctrine of the illusory nature of the universe.

There is a unity of purpose running through the entire book *i.e.*, the refutation of the Advaitin's conception of illusoriness of the universe. Several other issues are brought into the ambit of discussion, which have no intimate connection with the refutation of the illusory nature of the universe, the central theme of the book. It is the most compact, short and illuminating polemical tract of Dvaita Vedānta. Two printed editions of this book are available. (1) The Kumbakonam edition with the commentary of S'rī Rāghavendra published by T. R. Krishnnamachariar. (2) The Belgaum edition with three commentaries from Sri Raghavendra, S'rīnivāsatīrtha and Ubbarjīacār. A faithful rendering of the text into English is attempted here, to enable students of Vedānta to have an idea of the dialectics of Dvaita Vedānta.

These arguments have been met by Advaitins in several works of note: the *Bhedadhikkāra* of Nṛsimhās'ramin, the *Advaitamukura* of Rangarāja, and the *Advaitasidhi* of Madhusūdana Saras'vatī. A consideration of these refutations will have to be reserved for another time and place.

Benares Hindu University
15th April 1943

P. NAGARAJA RAO

ACKNOWLEDGMENTS

This volume was prepared by me while I was a Research Fellow of the Madras University in 1938 and 1939 under the able guidance and supervision of the late lamented Mr. Suryanarayana Sastri, Head of the Department of Indian Philosophy in the University of Madras. My acknowledgments are due to the University of Madras for having given me the facility for the preparation of the work and for the permission to publish it, and also to Dr. G. Srinivasa Murti, Hon. Director of the Adyar Library, for having kindly consented to publish the work in the Adyar Library Series. My special thanks are due to Dr. C. Kunhan Raja, Head of the Department of Sanskrit, University of Madras for having seen the book through the press and for having written his kind Foreword. I am deeply indebted to my revered teachers Kowligi Yedhunathachar and Yallatur Narasimhachar for having taught me the several texts of Dvaita Vedānta.

P. N. R.

॥ श्रीः ॥

श्रीमद्धनुमद्भीममध्वान्तर्गतरामकृष्णवेदव्यासात्मकलक्ष्मीहयग्रीवाय नमः

वादावली

नमोऽगणितकल्याणगुणपूर्णाय विष्णवे ।
सत्याशेषजगज्जन्मपूर्वकर्त्रे मुरद्विषे ॥ १ ॥

२. ननु कथं सत्यता जगतोऽङ्गीकाराधिकारिणी? विमतं मिथ्या दृश्यत्वात्, जडत्वात्, परिच्छिन्नत्वात्, शुक्तिरजतवत् इत्यनुमानविरोधात्—इति ।

VĀDĀVALĪ

I

1. Obeisance to Lord Viṣṇu, filled with infinite auspicious attributes, the agent of creation and the rest (sustentation etc.) of the entire (absolutely) real universe, and the destroyer of (the demon) Mura.

II

2. Now, how can the (absolute) reality of the universe be worthy of acceptance, inasmuch as there is conflict of it with the inference "what is under dispute

३. नैवम्; मिथ्यात्वानिरुक्तेः। तत् किमनिर्वचनीयत्वं वा? असत्त्वं वा? सद्विविक्तत्वं वा? प्रमाणाविषयत्वं वा? अप्रमाणविषयत्वं वा? अविद्यातत्कार्ययोरन्यतरत्वं वा? स्वात्यन्ताभावसमानाधिकरणतया प्रतीयमानत्वं वा?

४. नाद्यः; विकल्पासहत्वात्। तथाहि—अनिर्वचनीयत्वं किं निर्वचनविरहो वा? निर्वाच्यविरहो वा?

(the world) is illusory, because it is cognisable, because it is inert and because it is finite, like the shell-silver?"

III

3. (The siddhāntin replies) It is not so, for, the illusoriness (referred to) is undefined. (The siddhāntin resolves the term illusoriness into seven alternatives and examines each in detail) (1) Is it (*i.e.*, illusoriness) indeterminability, (2) or unreality, (3) or difference from the real, (4) or not being the content of valid cognition, (5) or being the content of invalid cognition, (6) or being either nescience or a product thereof, (7) or being cognised as in apposition with its own absolute non-existence?

IV

4. (The siddhāntin replies that not one of the alternatives is tenable). Not the first, since it cannot stand analysis. It is thus; is 'being indeterminable', equivalent to not having determination, or not having that which is determinable?

५. नाद्यः ; स्वाभ्युपगतव्यवहारविषयत्वविरोधात् ।

६. द्वितीये सत्त्वविरहो वा ? असत्त्वविरहो वा ? नाद्यः ; असतोऽनिर्वाच्यतापातात् । नोत्तरः ; ब्रह्मणोऽनिर्वाच्यतापातात् ।

७. अथ सदसद्वैलक्षण्यमनिर्वाच्यत्वं इति मतम्, तदास्माभिर्जगतः सदसद्रूपतानभ्युपगमात् सिद्धसाधनता ।

८. अथ प्रत्येकमुभयवैलक्षण्यं विवक्षितम्, तथाप्यसद्ब्रह्मवैलक्षण्याभ्युपगमेन प्रस्तुतदोषानिस्तारः ।

5. It cannot be the first, because it is opposed to what is admitted by (the Advaitin) himself, *viz.*, being the object of empirical usage.

6. If it is the second, then is it lack of reality, or lack of unreality? Not the first, because of the contingence of indeterminability of the unreal. Not the latter because of the contingence of the indeterminability of Brahman.

7. If (the Advaitin) opines that indeterminability is to be different from the real and the unreal, since we do not admit of the universe the character of the real-and-the-unreal, there is (the defect of) the establishment of the established.

8. If what is intended be the difference from each of the two individually, even then because of (the siddhāntin's) admission of the difference (of the universe) from the unreal and Brahman, the alleged defect is not got over.

९. एतेन सदसत्त्वानधिकरणत्वमनिर्वचनीयत्वमित्यपास्तम् ।

१०. प्रत्येकं सदसत्त्वाभ्यां विचारपदवीं न यत् ।
गाहते तदनिर्वाच्यमाहुर्वेदान्तवेदिनः ॥

इति चेन्न; तादृशवस्तुनोऽसिद्धत्वेनाप्रसिद्धविशेषणत्वात् ।

११. असत्त्वविरहे सत्त्वस्य, सत्त्वविरहेऽसत्त्वस्य नियतत्वेनोभय-विरहितत्वं व्याहतमेव ।

१२. ननु निषेधसमुच्चयस्य तात्त्विकत्वानभ्युपगमान्न व्याघातः ।

9. (The siddhāntin adds) By this (refutation, the above interpretation of) indeterminability as not being the substrate of reality and unreality (also) stands refuted.

10. (The Advaitin maintains)

> " That which is not able to be introduced into an inquiry either as real, or as unreal, this the learned Vedāntins call indeterminable ".

If this be said, no; since no such entity is established, there is (the defect of) non-established qualification.

11. Since reality is invariable where there is no unreality, and unreality where there is no reality, to be devoid of both is certainly self-contradictory.

12. (The Advaitin answers) Now because of the non-acceptance of the reality of a combination of negations, there is no contradiction.

१३. तत्तत्प्रतियोगिदुर्निरूपतामात्रप्रकटनाय तत्तद्विलक्षणताभिलापादिति चेन्न; तथा सति तस्यानिर्वचनीयतापातात्।

१४. यथा खलु सत्त्वासत्त्वे भवन्मते दुर्निरूपत्वान्न जगतो विद्येते, तथानिर्वचनीयताया अपि दुर्निरूपत्वेन तदभावो ध्रुवः स्यात्।

१५. असत्त्वविरहे सत्त्वम् इत्यादिव्याप्त्यसिद्धेर्न व्याहतिरिति चेन्न; आत्मादौ व्याप्तिसम्भवात्।

१६. तत्रात्मतत्त्वप्रयुक्तं सत्त्वमिति चेत्—किं तदात्मत्वम्?

13. "It is to explain only the indeterminable nature of the respective counter-correlates, that the differences from each are stated (of the universe)". If this be said, no (says the siddhāntin). For in that case there is the contingence of that (difference from the real and the unreal) becoming indeterminable.

14. Just as in your school, reality and unreality, because of the difficulty of determination, do not exist for the universe, even so indeterminability too being difficult of determination, the non-existence of that (in the universe) would be certain.

15. If it be said that there is no contradiction, because of the non-establishment of pervasions like "there is reality where there is no unreality" (the siddhāntin replies) no, for pervasion is possible in the case of the self (Ātman) etc.

V

16. If it be said (by the Advaitin) that reality there is due to selfhood (Ātmatva), then what is that

घटादिव्यावृत्ता आत्मवृत्तिर्जातिर्वा? किं वा सत्त्वं? उताबाध्यत्वम्? ज्ञानत्वं वा? ज्ञानाधारत्वं वा? स्वप्रकाशत्वं वा? आत्मपदवाच्यत्वं वा? तल्लक्ष्यत्वं वा?

१७. नाद्यः; आत्मन एकत्वेन तत्र जातेरयोगात्। कल्पितात्मभेदसद्भावान्नैवमिति चेन्न; कल्पितात्मनां पक्षनिक्षिप्ततया तस्यानुपाधित्वात्।

१८. न द्वितीयः; साध्याविशिष्टत्वात्।

१९. न तृतीयः; असति व्यभिचारात। तस्यापि बाध्यत्वे नासत्त्वस्यास्ति बाधकं इत्यात्मवचनविरोधात्।

selfhood? (1) Is it a generality excluded from pot etc., and present in the self, (2) or reality, (3) or unsublatability, (4) or to be the nature of knowledge, (5) or to be the substrate of knowledge, (6) or to be self-luminous, (7) or to be the express sense of the term self (Ātman) (8) or to be its secondary sense?

17. Not the first, as, the self being one, there is no possibility of a generality (jāti) in it. If it be said that because of the existence of assumptive differences of the self it is not thus (the impossibility of generality), no (says the siddhāntin); for, inasmuch as the assumptive self is included in the subject (of the syllogism), it cannot be an adjunct.

18. Not the second, because of the non-difference (of the probans) from the probandum.

19. Not the third, because of the inconstancy (of the probans) in respect of the unreal. If that be also sublatable, there is contradiction of one's own words "there is no sublater for the unreal."

२०. न चतुर्थः; पक्षैकदेशाव्यावृत्तेः।

२१. न पञ्चमः; आत्मन्यभावात्। तद्वतस्तस्य पक्षनिक्षेपात्।

२२. न षष्ठः; स्वप्रकाशताया उपर्यपाकार्यत्वात्।

२३. न सप्तमः; आत्मन्यभावात्। नान्त्यः; पक्षाव्यावृत्तेः।

२४. न च वाच्यम्—आत्मादौ न विकल्पोऽवकल्पते, तस्य तवापि सिद्धत्वादिति। अस्माभिरुक्तप्रकारान्यतरस्वीकारेऽपि त्वन्मते दोषग्रासानिस्तारात्।

20. Not the fourth, because it is not absent from a part of the subject.

21. Not the fifth, because it is non-existent in the self; for this (self) which possesses that (knowledge) gets included in the subject.

22. Not the sixth, since self-luminosity is to be refuted later.

23. Not the seventh, because it is non-existent in the self (in as much as for the Advaitin, the self is not the express sense of any word, not even of Ātman). It is not the last, because it is not absent from the subject, (as there even non-self may be the secondary sense of Ātman).

24. Nor should it be said, that it is not proper to analyse (the term) Ātman (self) etc., because that is established for you (the Dvaitins) also. Though we (the Dvaitins) admit any one of the stated alternatives, for you, the taint of defect (in accepting any of these) is inescapable.

२५. तस्मादसत्त्वविरहे सत्त्वमित्यादिव्याप्तिसिद्धेरुभयविरहित्वं व्याहतमेवेति सिद्धम् ।

२६. किञ्च न सदसद्विलक्षणत्वे मानम् ।

२७. विवादपदं सदसद्विलक्षणमिति प्रतिज्ञायां पक्षस्याप्रसिद्धविशेषणत्वप्रसङ्गात् ।

२८. सत्त्वासत्त्वे एकवस्तुनिष्ठात्यन्ताभावप्रतियोगिनी, धर्मत्वात्, रूपरसवत् इत्यनुमाने वस्तुशब्दस्य सच्छब्दपर्यायत्वात् सत्त्वं सन्निष्ठात्यन्ताभावप्रतियोगीति व्याघातः ।

25. Therefore, through the establishment of pervasions like "where there is no unreality, there is reality", it is established that absence of both is certainly self-contradictory.

VI

26. (The siddhāntin points out that there is no authority in respect of indeterminability). Again in respect of the difference from the real and the unreal there is no authority.

27. In the proposition 'what is under dispute is different from the real and the unreal' (if inference be suggested as the authority) there is the contingence of non-established qualification in respect of the subject.

28. In the inference "reality and unreality are the counter-correlates of the absolute non-existence located in a single entity, because they are attributes, like colour and taste," because the term entity (vastu) is synonymous with the word reality (sat), there is the

२९. प्रमेयत्वाभिधेयत्वादावनैकान्तिकश्च ।

३०. अविरुद्धत्वमुपाधिश्च ।

३१. किञ्च घटत्वाघटत्वे एकधर्मनिष्ठात्यन्ताभावप्रतियोगिनी, धर्मत्वात्, रूपरसवत् इत्याभाससमानयोगक्षेमश्च ।

३२. सच्चेन्न बाध्येत ; असच्चेन्न प्रतीयेत इत्यर्थापत्तिरेवानिर्वचनीये प्रमाणमिति चेन्न ;

३३. सच्चेन्न बाध्येत इत्यत्र किमिदं सत् विवक्षितम् ? किं सत्तायुक्तम् ? अथाबाध्यम् ? उत ब्रह्मस्वरूपम् ?

contradiction—reality is the counter-correlate of the absolute non-existence located in reality."

29. And there is the inconstancy (of the probans) in respect of knowability and nameability.

30. And (further) being non-contradictory is an adjunct (in the example cited).

31. Besides, there is parity of welfare in respect of fallaciousness with (the following inference): Potness and non-potness are the counter-correlates of the absolute non-existence located in one substrate, because they are attributes like colour and taste.

32. "If it be real it could not be sublated; if it be unreal it could not be cognised"; if it be said, that such a presumptive implication is the authority for the indeterminable, no (answers the siddhāntin).

33. In the (statement) "if it be real, it could not be sublated", what is it that is intended by this (term) real? (1) is it what possesses reality (2) or the unsublatable, (3) or the nature of Brahman?

३४. नाद्यः; सत्तायुक्तस्य प्रपञ्चस्य भवन्मते बाध्यतया यत् सत् तत् अबाध्यमिति व्याप्त्यसिद्धेः ।

३५. न द्वितीयः; यदबाध्यं तदबाध्यमिति साध्याविशिष्टत्वात् ।

३६. न तृतियः; सिद्धसाधनत्वात् ।

३७. असत्त्वेन प्रतीयेत इत्यत्रासतोऽसत्त्वेन प्रतीतिर्निषिध्यते सत्त्वेन वा ।

३८. आद्ये असद्व्यवहारलोपप्रसङ्गः । द्वितीये भ्रान्तिव्यवहार-लोपप्रसङ्गः ।

34. Not the first; as the universe possessing reality is according to your school (Advaita) sublatable, there is non-establishment of the pervasion "what is real is not sublatable".

35. Not the second, because of the non-difference (of the subject) from the probandum (resulting from the statement) "that which is not sublatable is not sublatable."

36. Not the third, because of the establishment of the established (it is established for the Dvaitin, that the nature of Brahman is unsublatable).

37. "If it be unreal, it could not be cognised". In this (statement) is it that the cognition of the unreal as unreal is denied, or (the cognition of the unreal) as real.

38. In the first case, there is the contingence of the failure of empirical usage (*i.e.*, verbal designation) in respect of the unreal. In the second case there is the contingence of the failure of empirical usage in respect of delusion.

३९. प्रकृतादन्यात्मना प्रतीतेरेव भ्रान्तित्वात्। तत्र चान्याकारस्यासतः सत्त्वेन प्रतिभासाङ्गीकारात् तस्यानिर्वचनीयत्वं ब्रूम इति चेन्न।

४०. तदपि किं प्रकृतेनैव रूपेण प्रतीयते भ्रान्तावन्याकारेण वा? आद्ये भ्रान्तिव्यवहारलोपप्रसङ्गः।

४१. द्वितीयेऽसतस्सत्त्वेन प्रतीतिरनिवार्या। अथ तस्याप्यनिर्वचनीयत्वं मन्यसे, तर्ह्यनवस्था।

४२. तथा च निर्णयदर्शनं दुश्शकं प्रसज्येत।

39. For it is only the cognition (of an object) as of a nature other than its own that is delusion. "And there there is accepted the appearance as real of what is different in nature *i.e.*, the unreal. Hence we declare the indeterminability of that (delusion)" If this be said, no (says the siddhāntin).

40. In that delusive cognition, is that (indeterminability) too cognised as having its own nature or as of another nature? In the first case there is the contingence of failure of the empirical usage in respect of delusion.

41. In the second case, there is no getting over the cognition of the unreal as real. If that too be considered indeterminable, then there would be infinite regress.

42. Thus there is the contingence of the impossibility of sighting ascertainment (in respect of indeterminability).

४३. न द्वितीयः ; अपदर्शनत्वात् ।

४४. न तृतीयः ; विचारागोचरत्वात् । तथाहि—कासौ सद्विविक्तता नाम ?

४५. किं परजातिविरहः ? अब्रह्मत्वं वा ? असत्त्वं वा ; अबाध्येतरत्वं वा ?

४६. नाद्यः ; तेनापि जगति जातेरनिराकरणात् ।

४७. न द्वितीयः ; सिद्धसाधनत्वात् ।

४८. न तृतीयः ; अपसिद्धान्तात् ।

VII

43. Not the second, becaue it is opposed to their school of thought.

VIII

44. Not the third, because it is beyond the sphere of inquiry. It is thus :—What is this which is called "being different from the real" ?

45. Is it to lack the summum genus, or to be not-Brahman, or to be unreal, or to be other than the non-sublatable ?

46. Not the first, because by him (who advocates illusoriness) too has not been rejected (the presence of) generality in the universe.

47. Not the second, because of (the defect of) the establishment of the established. (The statement that the universe is not Brahman is accepted by the Dvaitin).

48. Not the third, because it is opposed to their own doctrine.

४९. चतुर्थोऽपि ब्रह्मेतरत्वाभ्युपगमेन सिद्धसाधनत्वात् ।

५०. अबाध्येतरत्वं नाम बाध्यत्वमिति चेन्न ; बाध्यत्वानिरूपणात् ।

५१. तत्किमन्यथाज्ञातस्य सम्यग्ज्ञातत्वं ? प्रतिपन्नोपाधौ निषेधप्रतियोगित्वं वा ।

५२. नाद्यः ; सिद्धसाधनत्वात् । अस्माभिरपि सर्वमनिर्वचनीयमित्याद्यन्यथाज्ञातस्य जगतो यथावज्ज्ञातताभ्युपगमात् ।

५३. द्वितीये किमेकदेशकालप्रतिपन्नस्य कालान्तरादौ निषेधप्रतियोगित्वम् ? उत त्रिकालाखिलदेशनिषेधप्रतियोगित्वम् ?

49. Since in the fourth too, because of the acceptance of the difference (of the universe) from Brahman, there is (the defect) of the establishment of the established, (it is not so).

50. If it be said that "to be other than unsublatable" is what is called sublatability, no (says the siddhāntin), because sublatability is unexplained.

51. Does that (sublatability) consist in an object otherwise (*i.e.* erroneously) cognised being validly cognised, or in being the counter-correlate of negation in the locus of cognition (pratipannopādhi) ?

52. Not the first, because of (the defect) of the establishment of the established; for in respect of the universe known (to you) otherwise (*i.e.* erroneously) in the form "everything is indeterminable" and so on, (valid) knowledge as it is is admitted even by us.

53. In the second (alternative), is it to be the counter-correlate of the negation at some other time etc., in respect of what has been cognised at some

५४. नाद्यः ; अंशे सिद्धसाधनत्वात् ।

५५. रीत्यन्तरेणानित्यत्वादेरेवोक्तत्वात् ।

५६. न द्वितीयः ; नित्यसर्वगतयोः कालाकाशयोस्तादृशबाधप्रतिज्ञाने व्याघातात् ।

५७. का चेयं प्रतिपन्नता नाम ? प्रमाणप्रतिपन्नता ? भ्रान्तिप्रतिपन्नता वा ?

५८. नाद्यः ; प्रमाणप्रतिपन्नस्य त्रिकालाखिलदेशनिषेधप्रतियोगितासाधनेऽतिप्रसङ्गात् ।

particular place and time, or is it to be the counter-correlate of the negation in respect of all three times and all places ?

54. Not the first, because of (the defect) of the establishment of the established in respect of a part (of the subject).

55. For, 'it is only non-eternality etc. that is stated in another mode (as sublatability).

56. Not the second, because there is contradiction in premising that kind of sublatability in respect of the eternal and omnipresent ether (Ākāśa) and time.

57. What is this which is called "being cognised"? Is it to be validly cognised or delusively cognised ?

58. Not the first, because in the case of the validly cognised, there is undue extension in establishing that it is the counter-correlate of the negation in respect of all three times, and all places.

५९. द्वितीये वक्तव्यम्—कोऽयं निषेधः? अभाववेदनम्, सद्विविक्तत्ववेदनं वा?

६०. नाद्यः; अत्यन्तासत्त्वापातात्। न द्वितीयः; तस्यैवाद्याप्यनिरूपणात्।

६१. न चतुर्थः; विचारागोचरत्वात्। तथाहि—प्रमाणाविषयत्वं नाम यत्किञ्चित्प्रमाणाविषयत्वं वा? प्रमाणमात्राविषयत्वं वा?

६२. नाद्यः; गन्धादेः श्रोत्राद्यविषयतासिध्या सिद्धसाधनत्वात्।

59. In the second case, it has to be said, "what is this negation?" Is it cognition of non-existence, or cognition of being other than real?

60. Not the first, because of the contingence of absolute unreality. Not the second, because that itself (being other than the real) is still unexplained.

IX

61. Not the fourth, because it is beyond the sphere of inquiry. It is thus. The term "not being the object of a means of valid knowledge", does it mean "not being the object of some one means of valid knowledge" or "not being the object of means of valid knowledge in general"?

62. Not the first, because of (the defect) of the establishment of the established through the establishment (of the fact) of odour etc. being not the object of the sense of hearing etc.

६३. न द्वितीयः ; ब्रह्मणोऽपि मिथ्यात्वापातात् ।

६४. प्रमाणाविषयत्वे प्रपञ्चस्य तत्पक्षीकरणायोगाच्च ।

६५. अतत्त्वावेदकप्रत्यक्षादिसिद्धतया पक्षीकरणमुपपन्नमिति चेन्न ; प्रत्यक्षादेरतत्त्वावेदकत्वे मानाभावात् ।

६६. विषयस्यासत्त्वादेव तत्सिद्धिरिति चेत्—तदेव कुतः ?

६७. किञ्चातत्त्वावेदकं प्रमाणं चेति व्याघातः ।

६८. अतत्त्वावेदकं प्रमाणं चेत्—शुक्तिरजतज्ञानमपि प्रमाणं

63. Not the second, because of the contingence of illusoriness even of Brahman.

64. And (it is also so) because, if the universe be not an object of any means of valid knowledge, there is the impossibility of making that (universe) the subject (in a syllogism).

65. If it be said that it is intelligible to make that the subject as established by perception, etc., which make known the non-real, no (says the siddhāntin), because there is no authority (to the effect) that perception, etc., make known the non-real.

66. (If the Advaitin contends) that it (the cognition of non-real objects by perception) is established even because of the unreality of the content, whence is this (the unreality of the objects) itself (known)?

67. Further, there is contradiction in (the statement) that (perception) makes known the non-real and is (yet) a means of valid knowledge.

68. If that which makes known the non-real be a means of valid knowledge, then, why should not the

किं न स्यात्? अतत्त्वावेदकत्वाविशेषात्। प्रमाणं चेत्—नातत्त्वावेदकम्, अद्वैतवाक्यवत्।

६९. न पञ्चमः; सर्वमनिर्वचनीयम्, क्षणिकम्, ब्रह्माकार्यम्, इत्याद्यप्रमाणविषयताभ्युपगमेन सिद्धसाधनत्वात्।

७०. भ्रमप्रतीतत्वं विवक्षितमिति चेत्—तथा सति तस्यासत्त्वेन सिद्धान्तविरोधः।

७१. न षष्ठः; केयमविद्या नाम? अनाद्यनिर्वाच्या वा? अनादिभावरूपत्वे सति विज्ञानविलाप्या वा? भ्रमोपादानं वा?

cognition of shell-silver too be a valid knowledge, since there is no distinction in respect of making known the non-real. If it is a means of valid knowledge, it does not make known the non-real, like the texts about non-duality.

X

69. Not the fifth, because when there is admitted (the universe) being the object of what is not a means of valid knowledge, *e.g.* "all things are indeterminable, momentary, not produced by Brahman" etc., there is (the defect of) the establishment of the established.

70. If it be said that what is intended is being delusively cognised, in that case that (content of the delusive cognition) being unreal, there is opposition to (your) doctrine.

XI

71. Not the sixth. What is this which is called nescience? Is it what is begining produced detminable,

७२. नाद्यः; अनिर्वाच्यासिध्याप्रसिद्धविशेषणत्वात्। आकाशादौ लक्षणस्यातिव्याप्तेश्च।

७३. ब्रह्मव्यतिरिक्तस्यानादित्वानभ्युपगमान्नैवमिति चेत्—एवं तर्हि लक्षणस्यासम्भवः।

७४. न द्वितीयः; अनादित्वस्यासम्भवित्वात्। अनादिभावरूपस्य विज्ञानविलापनासम्भवाच्च, ब्रह्मवत्।

७५. भावाभावविलक्षणाविद्याया अभावविलक्षणतामात्रेण भावत्वोपचारादात्मवदनादिभावत्वेनानिवर्त्यत्वानुमानानुपपत्तिरिति चेन्न।

or is it that which, while in form a beginningless existent, is destructible by cognition, or is it the material cause of delusion?

72. Not the first, because of the (defect of) non-established qualification resulting from the non-establishment of indeterminability, also because the definition is over-pervasive in respect of ether (ākāśa) etc.

73. If it be said that because of the non-acceptance of beginninglessness (in respect of) objects different from Brahman, it is not so, (*i.e.*, there is no over-pervasion), in that case there is inapplicability of the definition.

74. Not the second, because of the impossibility of beginninglessness, also because, for what in form is a beginningless existent, destruction by cognition is not possible, like Brahman.

75. "There is unintelligibility of the inference of non-destructibility (by cognition) on the ground of being a beginningless entity, like the self, for the

७६. अभावविलक्षणतामात्रेणाप्यनादेरनिवर्त्यत्वानुमानसम्भवात् ।

७७. न चात्मत्वादिरुपाधिः, अत्यन्तासति व्यभिचारात् ।

७८. न तृतीयः, भ्रमशब्देनार्थो ज्ञानं वा ?

७९. नाद्यः ; पदार्थस्यासत्त्वेन तदुपादानताया असम्भवात् ।

८०. न द्वितीयः ; अन्तःकरणेऽतिव्याप्तेः । भ्रमस्याविद्योपादानकताभावेनासम्भवित्वाच्च ।

nescience that is different from the existent and the non-existent, through the mere figurative reference as the existent because of its difference from non-existent." If this be said, it is not so.

76. (The siddhāntin replies.) Even through the mere difference from the non-existent, there is the possibility of the inference of non-destructibility (by cognition) for what is beginningless.

77. Nor is self-hood, etc., an adjunct (limiting the pervasion), because there is inconstancy (of the probans) in respect of the absolutely non-existent.

78. Not the third. By the word delusion (what is it that is meant)—the content or the cognition ?

79. Not the first; because, the content (of the delusive cognition) being unreal, being its material cause is not possible.

80. Not the second, because of over-pervasion in respect of internal organ, and because there is inapplicability (of the definition), since delusion has not nescience for its material cause.

८१. तदनुपादानत्वे सत्यत्वं स्यादिति चेत्—स्यादेव ।

८२. तथा सति प्रमाणज्ञानवदेव विषयापहारलक्षणबाधस्याप्यप्रसङ्ग इति चेन्न ।

८३. तव व्याप्त्यसिद्धेः । तत्त्वावेदकस्यापि त्वयाविद्यकत्वाभ्युपगमात् ।

८४. एतावन्तं कालं रजतमभात् इत्यनुभवविरोधाच्च ।

८५. अनिर्वचनीयस्यापि भ्रमस्याभावविलक्षणतया तथात्वेनानुसन्धानोपपत्तिरिति चेन्न ।

81. If it be said that, if it (nescience) were not material cause, there would be reality (of the delusive content), (the siddhāntin replies), "that certainly would be so".

82. "If it (the delusion-content) be so (real), there is no contingence of sublation too consisting in privation of the content (of the delusive cognition) even as in the case of valid cognition." If this be said, no (says the siddhāntin).

83. For there is non-establishment of your (Advaitin's) pervasion, (the pervasion is between the reality of the object and the reality of the cognition) because of your admission that even what makes known the real is of the nature of nescience.

84. And (it is so) because there is conflict with this experience—"for this much time the silver was manifest".

85. If it be said that, since even the indeterminable delusion is different from non-existence, there is

८६. स्वरूपसत एवासीदिति प्रतिसन्धानात् ।

८७. एतावन्तं कालमिहादर्शे मुखमासीत्, स्फटिकश्च लोहित आसीत् इत्याद्यनुसन्धानान्नैवमिति चेत् ।

८८. एतावन्तं कालं मुखमद्राक्षम् इत्येवानुसन्धानेनानुसन्धानान्तरे विवादात् ।

८९. अविद्यायां चैवंविधायां किं प्रमाणम् ?

९०. देवदत्तप्रमा तत्स्थप्रमाप्रागभावातिरेकिणोऽनादेर्ध्वंसिका; प्रमात्वात्; अविगीतप्रमा यथा इत्यनुमानं मानमिति चेन्न ।

intelligibility of the recollection in that form, it is not so (says the siddhāntin).

86. For there is recollection in the form "it did exist" only in the case of what is real in its own nature.

87. "For this much time, my face was here in the mirror, and the crystal was red." Because of such recollections, it is not so (as stated above). If it be said thus (no).

88. For the recollection is only in the form "for this much time I saw (my) face"; therefore there is dispute as to any other recollection.

XII

89. What is the authority with reference to the nescience of such a nature?

90. (The Advaitin cites inference as the authority for the positive nature of nescience). If it be said that the inference, "Devadatta's valid cognition is the

९१. घटोऽयम् एतद्धटप्रागभावव्यतिरिक्तानादेर्निवर्तकः; घटत्वात्; घटान्तरवत् इत्याभाससमानयोगक्षेमत्वात्।

९२. एतेन—विगीतो भ्रमः एतज्जनकाबाध्यातिरिक्तोपादानकः; विभ्रमत्वात्; सम्प्रतिपन्नवत् इति च निरस्तम्। अनादित्वप्रमानिवर्त्यत्वयोर्विरोधाच्च।

९३. देवदत्तप्रमा देवदत्तगतैतत्प्रमाप्रागभावातिरिक्तानादेर्निवर्तिका न भवति; प्रमात्वात्; सम्प्रतिपन्नवत् इति सत्प्रतिपक्षता च।

destroyer of that which (1) is other than the prior non-existence of valid cognition located in that (Devadatta) and (2) is beginningless, because it is a valid cognition, like undisputed valid cognition", is the authority, no (says the siddhāntin).

91. For there is parity of welfare in respect of fallaciousness with (the following inference); "This pot is the destroyer of what is different from the prior non-existence of this pot and is beginningless, because it is a pot, like another pot."

92. And by this is (the inference) refuted: "The delusion under dispute has for material cause something other than that which produces it and is unsublatable, because it is a delusion, like the admitted (delusion)." And (it is so) because there is conflict between beginninglessness and destruction by valid cognition.

93. There is the (following) counter-probans, "Devadatta's valid cognition is not the destroyer of that which (1) is other than the prior non-existence of

९४. अथ प्रमाणज्ञानं स्वप्रागभावव्यतिरिक्तस्वविषयावरणस्वनिवर्त्यस्वदेशगतवस्त्वन्तरपूर्वकम्; अप्रकाशितार्थप्रकाशकत्वात्; अन्धकारे प्रथमोत्पन्नप्रदीपप्रभावात् इत्यनुमानं मानमस्तु।

९५. अत्र च प्रमाणज्ञानं वस्त्वन्तरपूर्वकमित्युक्ते स्वप्रागभावेन सिद्धसाधनता। तन्निवृत्त्यर्थं स्वप्रागभावव्यतिरिक्तेति पदम्।

९६. तथापि स्वप्रागभावव्यतिरिक्तस्वजनकसामग्र्या सिद्धसाधनम्। तन्निवृत्त्यर्थं स्वविषयावरणेति पदम्।

this valid cognition located in that (Devadatta) and (2) is beginningless, because it is a valid cognition, like the admitted (cognition)."

94. Then, let this inference be the authority: "Valid cognition has as antecedent some other entity which is (1) other than its own prior non-existence, (2) the obscurer of its own content, (3) removable by itself and (4) present in its own locus, because it is the manifestor of an object that was not manifested, like the light of a lamp as it first comes into existence from darkness.

95. And here, if it be said that valid cognition has some other entity as antecedent there would be (the defect of) the establishment of the established, having regard to prior non-existence. In order to remove it, there are the words "other than its own prior non-existence."

96. Even then (after defining valid cognition as that which has as antecedent some other entity other than its own prior non-existence) there is (the defect

९७. तथाप्यदृष्टेन सिद्धसाधनम्। तन्निवृत्त्यर्थं स्वनिवर्त्त्येति पदम्।

९८. अर्थान्तरनिवृत्तये आत्माश्रिताज्ञानसिद्ध्यै च स्वदेशेति पदमिति।

९९. नानेनानुमानेन त्वदभिमताज्ञानसिद्धिः। जडेऽज्ञानानभ्युपगमेनान्तःकरणवृत्तिलक्षणप्रमाणज्ञानानां तथाविधवस्तुपूर्वकत्वाभावेऽपि हेतोस्तत्र सद्भावादनैकान्तिकत्वात्।

of) the establishment of the established in respect of the causal aggregate which is other than the prior non-existence of (the valid cognition) itself and which produces it (valid cognition). In order to remove it there are the words " the obscurer of its own content."

97. Even thus there is (the defect of) the establishment of the established in respect of an unknown potency (adṛṣṭa). In order to remove that, there are the words, " removable by itself."

98. The words " (present in) its locus " are used in order to avoid the establishment of another (non-intended) object (*e.g.* non-cognisedness—ajñātatā) and to establish nescience which has the self (Ātman) for its locus.

99. There is no establishment of the nescience desired by you (the Advaitin) by such an inference (valid cognition, etc.). For, because of non-acceptance of nescience in respect of inert objects, for the valid cognitions which are of the nature of modifications of the (inert) internal organ, there is not the antecedence

१००. व्यर्थश्च स्वप्रागभावव्यतिरिक्तेति विशेषणम्। स्वनिवर्त्त्यविशेषणेनैव तद्व्यावृत्तेः।

१०१. न हि भावः स्वप्रागभावनिवर्तकः; अपि तु भावोत्पत्तिरेव तत्प्रागभावनिवर्तिका। भावाभावयोस्सहावस्थानविरोधात्। अतः स्वनिवर्त्त्यविशेषणेनैव स्वप्रागभावव्यावृत्तेर्व्यर्थं स्वप्रागभावव्यतिरिक्तेति विशेषणम्।

१०२. किञ्च सत्यतथाविधवस्तुपूर्वकत्वे साध्ये सिद्धसाधनम्। अनिर्वचनीयतथाविधवस्तुपूर्वकत्वे साध्ये साध्यविकलो दृष्टान्तः।

of an entity of the said description; yet since there is presence of the probans there, there is (the defect of) inconclusiveness (of the probans).

100. And the attribute "other than its own prior non-existence" is purposeless, for, that exclusion is secured even by the qualification "removable by itself."

101. The positive entity is not what destroys its own prior non-existence. On the contrary coming into existence of the positive entity is alone what destroys the prior non-existence, since there is contradiction in the co-existence of the existent and the non-existent. And thus, since the attribute "removable by itself" secures of itself the exclusion of its prior non-existence, the attribute "other than its own prior non-existence" is purposeless.

102. Besides, if the probandum be "being preceded by a real entity of that kind", there would be (the defect of) the establishment of the established. If the probandum be "being preceded by an indeterminable entity of that kind", the example would lack the probandum.

१०३. अविशेषिततथाविधवस्तुपूर्वकत्वे साध्येऽप्रसिद्धविशेषणता ।

१०४. प्रामाणिकाप्रामाणिकयोः साधारणधर्मस्याप्यप्रामाणिकत्वात् । अनिर्वचनीयस्य केनापि प्रमाणेनाप्रमितत्वात् । न हि शशविषाणगोविषाणयोर्विषाणत्वसामान्यमस्ति ।

१०५. ज्ञानप्रतिबन्धकपापस्य सिद्धतया सिद्धसाधनत्वं च । ज्ञाननिवर्त्यत्वात्तस्यापि ।

१०६. किञ्च किमिदं प्रकाशकत्वं नाम ? ज्ञापकत्वं वा ? ज्ञापकाप्यायकत्वं वा ? ज्ञानत्वं वा ।

103. If the probandum be "being preceded by an entity of that kind which (at the same time) is not particularised (as real or indeterminable)" there is (the defect) of non-established qualification.

104. For, an attribute common to both what is cognised as valid and what is cognised as invalid, is itself invalidly cogised (and) what is indeterminable is not validly cognised by any means of valid knowledge whatever. There is indeed no attribute, hornness, common to the horns of a hare and the horns of a cow.

105. Besides, through the establishment of demerit which obstructs cognition, there is (the defect of) the establishment of the established; for that too is removable by cognition.

106. Further, what is this which is called "being a manifestor"? Is it being the instrument of cognition

१०७. नाद्यः ; चक्षुरादौ व्यभिचारात् । दृष्टान्तस्य साधनविकलत्वाच्च । ज्ञाने ज्ञानकरणत्वाभावेनासिद्धेश्च ।

१०८. न द्वितीयः ; असिद्धेः । अञ्जनादौ व्यभिचाराच्च ।

१०९. न तृतीयः ; साधनविकलत्वाद्दृष्टान्तस्य ।

११०. न किञ्चिद्वेदिषमिति परामर्शसिद्धस्सौषुप्तिकानुभवोऽस्तु प्रमाणमिति चेन्न ; तस्य ज्ञानाभावविषयतयोपपत्तेः ।

or being accessory to the instrument of cognition, or being cognition ?

107. Not the first, because there is inconstancy (of the probans) in respect of the sense of sight etc., also because the example is devoid of the probans, and also because there is the non-establishment (of the probans) since in the case of cognition, there is no instrumentality to cognition.

108. Not the second, because of the non-establishment (of the probans,) and because there is also inconstancy (of the probans) in respect of collyrium (añjana) etc.

109. Not the third, since the example is devoid of the probans.

110. If it be said that there may be this means of valid knowledge, namely, the experience relating to sleep established by recollection (in the form) "I did not know anything", no (says the siddhāntin) ; for that (experience) is intelligible as having for content the non-existence of recognition.

१११. नन्वभावप्रतीतेर्धर्मिप्रतियोगिबोधपराधीनतया तदभावे तस्यानुभवितुमयोग्यत्वमिति चेन्न; साक्षिणा धर्मिप्रतियोगिग्रहणोपपत्तेः।

११२. यत्तु कश्चिदाह—नाज्ञानं ज्ञानाभावः, अभावमानागम्यत्वात् सम्प्रतिपन्नवत्।

११३. अभावो ह्यभावस्य प्रत्यक्षस्य वा विषयः। अज्ञानञ्च न मानगम्यम्, माननिवर्त्यत्वात्, सम्प्रतिपन्नवदिति।

११४. तदसत्; अज्ञानस्य मानगम्यत्वे तत्साधनायानुमानकथनायोगात्। एतन्मानगम्यत्वेन मानागम्यमिति व्याघातः।

111. "Now, the cognition of non-existence being dependent on the knowledge of the substrate and of the counter-correlate, in the absence of that (knowledge of the substrate and counter-correlate) that (non-existence) is not capable of being experienced"; if this be said, no; for the apprehension of both the substrate and the counter-correlate by the witness (self) is intelligible.

112. Some say "nescience is not the non-existence of cognition, because it is not cognised by the means of valid knowledge, negation (*i.e.*, anupalabdhi which makes known non-existence), like what is admitted.

113. Non-existence (in the probans) indeed is the content either of negation or of perception. And nescience is not cognised by any means of valid knowledge, because it is destroyed by a valid knowledge, like what is admitted.

114. This is not sound (says the siddhāntin); for, if nescience be not cognised by any means of valid

११५. फलव्याप्यताभावेऽपि वृत्तिव्याप्यतामात्रेण तत्रानुमानप्रवृत्तिरिति न युक्तम् । अज्ञानस्य वृत्तिव्याप्यतानङ्गीकारात् ।

११६. न च प्रमाणनिवर्त्यत्वस्य प्रमाणगम्यत्वेन व्याप्तिरस्ति, प्रत्यभिज्ञाप्रमाणनिवर्त्यस्य संस्कारस्य मानगम्यत्वात् ।

११७. न च त्वदुक्तमर्थं न जानामीत्यादिव्यवहारोऽत्यन्तसुप्ते ज्ञायमाने चाज्ञायमाने सम्भाव्यमानोऽज्ञानं गमयतीति युक्तम् ।

knowledge, the application of inference to establish it would be unreasonable. Being cognised by this means of valid knowledge, (to say) that it is not cognised by any means of valid knowledge is contradiction (in terms).

115. "Though there is non-existence of being pervaded by the fruit (of cognition *i.e.*, the reflection of consciousness in the cognition), even because of being pervaded by the psychosis, there is application of the inference"; this does not stand to reason (says the siddhāntin), because the pervasion of nescience by psychosis is not admitted.

116. Nor is there pervasion of "removability through a means of valid knowledge" by "non-cognisability through a means of valid knowledge", because the impressions that are removed by the means of valid knowledge, recognition, are cognised by a means of valid knowledge.

117. Nor does it stand to reason that nescience is made known by such empirical usage as "I know not the object mentioned by you" which is possible,

११८. किमत्र सर्वानुवादेन व्यवहारः? किं वा सामान्यतः?

११९. नाद्यः; तादृशव्यवहारस्यैवाभावात्। भावे वा त्वदुक्तं न प्रमाणतो जानामीत्येवंपरत्वोपपत्तेः। प्रतिवादिवाक्यादधिगतार्थस्यानुवाद-पुरस्सरं प्रमाणाभावेन निरसनदर्शनात्।

१२०. न च त्वदुक्ते प्रमाणज्ञानं मम नास्तीत्यस्य विशिष्टविषय-ज्ञानस्य प्रमाणत्वात्तद्विशेषणतयार्थस्यापि प्रमाणेनाधिगमात्स्ववचनव्याघात इति युक्तम्।

whether there is absolute sleep (where there is ignorance of the self) or cognition (of the self or of the object) or non-cognition.

118. Here, is there the empirical usage through restatement of every (particular) or in a general way?

119. Not the first, because there is no such empirical usage at all; or if there were, it would be intelligible as having for purport "I know not through a means of valid knowledge the object mentioned by you"; for (the proponent) is seen to restate it after comprehending the meaning from the opponent's sentences, and subsequently to refute it, as not having a a means of valid knowledge.

120. Nor does it stand to reason (to urge) that because the cognition of the qualified object "I have no valid cognition in respect of what is mentioned by you" is valid, the content too, being its qualification, is known by a means of valid knowledge, and that hence there is contradiction in one's own words.

१२१. एतत्प्रमाणज्ञानस्य प्रमाणाभावविषयत्वेऽपि तदर्थस्यानेतद्विषयत्वात् । अन्यथा भ्रमो ममासीदित्यादिप्रमाणज्ञानस्यापि विशिष्टभ्रमविषयतया भ्रमविषयस्यापि प्रामाणिकतापातात् ।

१२२. न द्वितीयः; सामान्यानुवादेन विशेषव्यवहारोपपत्तेः ।

१२३. विशेषस्याप्यधिगमानधिगमयोर्नैवं व्यवहार इति चेन्न; अस्ति कश्चिद्विशेष इति सामान्यतो ज्ञातत्वात् ।

१२४. किञ्च भावरूपाविद्याभ्युपगमेऽपि किं पूर्वमर्थो ज्ञातो न वा? सर्वथापि प्रश्नायोगः ।

121. For though this valid cognition too has for content the non-existence of a means of valid knowledge, the object of this (latter) is not the content of that (former). Otherwise the valid cognition "I experienced a delusion" having for its content a delusion about what is qualified, there is the contingent of the content of the delusion too becoming valid.

122. Not the second; for through reference in general terms (to what was said), there is intelligibility for the empirical usage (of ignorance) in respect of the particular.

123. If it be said that even in respect of the particular, there would not be such empirical usage, whether cognised or uncognised, it is not so (says the siddhāntin); for, it is known in a general way, "there is some particular".

124. Further, even if there is acceptance of nescience with a positive nature, is the content (of nescience)

१२५. अस्माकं तु सर्वं वस्तु ज्ञाततयाज्ञाततया वा साक्षिचैतन्यविषय एवेति प्रमाणज्ञानोदयात्प्रागज्ञातत्वविशेषितोऽर्थस्साक्षिसिद्धोऽनुवादगोचरो भवति च प्रश्नार्ह इति चेन्न ।

१२६. साक्षिसिद्धतयापि सिद्धेऽर्थे व्यवहारायोगात् ।

१२७. साक्षिणा ज्ञातेऽपि प्रमाणबुभुत्सया व्यवहार इति चेन्न; साक्षिसिद्धत्वे प्रमाणबुभुत्साया निष्फलत्वात् ।

known earlier or not? In no case can there be a question (about it).

125. "For us, (the Advaitins) all the objects whether as cognised or as not cognised are the contents of witness-consciousness; hence the content qualified by non-cognisedness prior to the rise of valid cognition is established by the witness-consciousness, is capable of being referred to and becomes capable of being questioned about." If this be said, no (replies the siddhāntin),

126. For in respect of a content, which is established even as established by the witness-consciousness, there cannot be the empirical usage (of ignorance).

127. If it be said that though it is cognised by witness-consciousness, there is the empirical usage because of the desire to know the means of valid knowledge, no; for in the case of that which is established by witness-consciousness the desire to know the means of valid knowledge is fruitless.

१२८. तथा च त्वयापि सामान्यतस्सिद्धोऽर्थो विशेषज्ञानायानूद्यते इति वक्तव्यम् ।

१२९. वयमपि समान्यतः साक्षिसिद्धस्य विशेषप्रमाणबुभुत्सया व्यवहारं ब्रूमः ।

१३०. तस्मान्नाविद्या निरूपणगोचरतामाचरतीति कुतस्तत्कार्यम्? कुतस्तरां चाविद्यातत्कार्ययोरन्यतरत्वस्य साध्यता सिध्यतीति ।

१३१. न च भावरूपाज्ञाननिराकरणे सिद्धान्तविरोधः, परन्यायेन परनिराकरणात् ।

128. And thus you (Advaitins) too must say that for the sake of the knowledge of the particular, what is established in general is referred to.

129. We (Dvaitins) too do say that the empirical usage (of ignorance) is because of the desire to know the means of valid knowledge for the particular in respect of that which is established in general by the witness-consciousness.

130. Therefore nescience does not come within the sphere of being demonstrated; hence how can it have any product? And still more, how can there be established the character of being the probandum either for nescience or for its product?

XIII

131. Nor by the refutation of nescience of a positive nature is there the defect "being opposed to one's final position," because there is refutation of the opponent (above) on the opponent's own principles."

१३२. न सप्तमः ; अत्यन्ताभावपदेनासत्त्वाभिप्रायेऽपसिद्धान्तः । तदतिरिक्तस्याप्रसिद्धत्वात् ।

१३३. भाववैलक्षण्यमिति चेत्—तर्हि तत एवासत्त्वापत्त्या नोक्तदोषनिवृत्तिः । तस्मान्न मिथ्यात्वनिरुक्तिः ।

१३४. नापि दृश्यत्वस्य । तथाहि—किमिदं दृश्यत्वम्? दृग्विषयत्वम्? अप्रकाशत्वं वा?

१३५. आद्ये किं दृग्वृत्तिरूपा चिद्रूपा वा?

XIV

132. Not the seventh ; if the word "absolute non-existence" is intended to mean unreality, then there is (the defect of) "opposition to one's own school of thought"; for, what is other than that is non-established.

133. If it is said that it (absolute non-existence) is "being different from the existent", then because of the contingence of unreality even from this, there is no removal of the said defect (the refutation of the indeterminability of illusoriness). Therefore there is no definition of illusoriness.

XV

134. Nor of cognisability (is there a definition) too. It is thus : what is this cognisability ? Is it being the content of cognition, or non-self-luminosity ?

135. In the first case, is the cognition of the form of psychosis, or of the form of consciousness ?

१३६. नाद्यः; आत्मन्यनैकान्त्यात्। तस्यापि वेदान्तजनितवृत्तिविषयत्वात्।

१३७. वृत्तिजनितफलासम्बन्धान्नानैकान्त्यमिति चेत्—फलं ज्ञातता व्यवहारो वा।

१३८. आद्ये घटादावपि तदभावादसिद्धिः। अतीतानागतनित्यानुमेयेषु ज्ञातताभावाद्भागासिद्धिश्च।

१३९. तथाहि—अवेद्यत्वे सत्यपरोक्षव्यवहारयोग्यत्वं स्वप्रकाशत्वमिति तल्लक्षणमभिदधता चित्सुखेनापरोक्षव्यवहारयोग्यताविशेषणकृत्या-

136. Not the first, because of inconclusiveness (of the probans) in respect of the self (Ātman); for that (self) too is the content of the psychosis arising from (the study of) Vedānta.

137. If it be said that, because of the non-relatedness to the fruit arising from psychoses, there is no inconclusiveness (of the probans), then is the fruit cognisedness or empirical usage?

138. In the first case, because of its (probans) non-existence even in pot, etc. there is the non-establishment (of the probans). Because of the non-existence of cognisedness in (objects that are) past, future and eternally to be inferred there is also partial non-establishment (of the probans in the subject).

139. It is thus. Citsukha, who states its definition "self-luminosity is capacity to be the object of empirical usage of immediacy, while not being the object of cognition", while explaining the function of the

भिधानप्रस्तावेऽभिहितम्—न चाविद्यात्वमित्येतावदेवास्तु तल्लक्षणमिति वाच्यम् । तथा सत्यतीतानागतनित्यानुमेयेषु चातिव्याप्तेः । फलव्याप्यतालक्षणवेद्यत्वस्य तत्राभावादिति ।

१४०. द्वितीये पुनरनैकान्त्यमेव । आत्मनोऽपि वृत्तिजन्यव्यवहारविषयत्वात् ।

१४१. चिद्रूपदृग्विषयत्वं तु घटादावस्माभिर्नाङ्गीक्रियते इति भागासिद्धिः ।

१४२. स्वप्रकाशत्वञ्च निर्वक्तव्यं यदभावो दृश्यत्वम् । अवेद्य-

qualification "capacity to be the object of empirical usage of immediacy" says thus: "it should not be said: let 'not being the object of cognition' alone be the definition; for if so there is over-pervasion in respect of (objects that are) past, future and eternally to be inferred; for 'being the object of cognition', consisting in being pervaded by the fruit, does not exist in these".

140. In the second case again, there is certainly inconclusiveness (of the probans), because the self (Ātman) too is the content of empirical usage generated by psychoses.

141. As for being the object of cognition of the nature of consciousness, since that is not admitted by us in the case of pot etc., there is partial non-establishment (of the probans).

142. And that self-luminosity whose non-existence is cognisability has to be defined. If that is said to be

त्वमिति चेत् - तर्हि वेद्यत्वं दृश्यत्वमित्युक्तं स्यात् । तथा च प्रागुक्तविकल्पदोषापातः ।

१४३. स्वव्यवहारे स्वातिरिक्तसंविदनपेक्षत्वं स्वप्रकाशत्वम्; तदभावो दृश्यत्वमिति चेत्—तर्ह्यात्मनोऽप्यद्वितीयव्यवहारे संविदन्तरापेक्षासद्भावाद्व्यभिचारः ।

१४४. निर्विकल्पकस्य व्यवहारे संविदन्तरानपेक्ष आत्मेति चेत्—तर्हि घटोऽपि तथैवेत्यसिद्धिः ।

"not being an object of cognition", then it turns out to be saying "cognisability is being an object of cognition." And thus there is the contingence of the defects from the analysis made earlier.

XVI

143. "Non-dependence on any consciousness other than itself for empirical usage in respect of itself is self-luminosity; its non-existence is cognisability." If this be said, then there is inconstancy (of the probans) in respect of the self which is dependent on a consciousness other than itself in respect of empirical usage as "non-dual".

144. If it be said that in the self there is the non-dependence on any consciousness other than itself, in respect of indeterminate empirical usage, then, because the (probans) pot is certainly like that, there is non-establishment of the probans.

१४५. घटे निर्विकल्पकव्यवहार एव नास्तीति चेत्—आत्मन्यपि स नास्त्येव ।

१४६. सुषुप्तावस्तीति चेन्न; तस्यापि निर्विकल्पकत्वे विवादात् ।

१४७. अवेद्यत्वे सत्यपरोक्षव्यवहारविषयत्वं स्वप्रकाशत्वमिति चेन्न; व्याहतत्वेनासम्भवित्वात् ।

१४८. कथञ्चिदव्याहतत्वेऽपि विशेषणाभावेन, उत विशेष्याभावेन, अथोभयाभावेन दृश्यत्वं निर्वक्तव्यम् ।

145. If it be urged that there is no indeterminate usage at all in respect of the pot, (then), it does not exist even in the case of the self.

146. If it be said that it is present in deep sleep, no (we reply) since the indeterminate nature of that too is under dispute.

XVII

147. If it be said that self-luminosity is "to be an object of empirical usage as directly cognised, while not being an object of cognition", no, since (the definition), being contradictory, is inapplicable.

148. Even if somehow or other it be (considered) non-contradictory, (then too) cognisability has to be defined through the non-existence of the qualification, or through the non-existence of the qualified, (*i.e.*, substrate) or through the non-existence of both.

१४९. तत्राद्येऽवेद्यत्वाभावो वेद्यत्वमेव हेतुरस्तु। किं विशेष्येण? तस्य चोक्तं दूषणम्।

१५०. द्वितीये स्वरूपासिद्धिः।

१५१. तृतीये व्यर्थविशेषणत्वम्, विशेष्यासिद्धिश्चेति।

१५२. किञ्च दृश्यत्वं प्रमाणतो वा भ्रान्त्या वा? नोभयमपि, अन्यतरासिद्धेः।

१५३. ननु सामान्यतः प्रयुक्तस्य हेतोर्विशेषविकल्पैर्निराकरणे सर्वानुमानाभावप्रसङ्गः।

149. Of these, in the first case, let (the qualification) "being the object of cognition," itself be the probans as non-existence of not being an object of cognition. What (is the use) of the qualified (*i.e.*, substrate)? And of this (procedure) the defect has already been mentioned.

150. In the second case, there is the non-establishment of the existence (of the probans in respect of part or whole of the subject).

151. In the third case, the qualification is futile; further, the qualified (substrate) is non-established.

XVIII

152. Again, is the cognisability through a means of valid knowledge, or through delusion. It is not both (of them), because of non-establishment of one or the other.

153. Now if the probans adduced in general is refuted through the analysis of the particular (forms)

१५४. तथाहि—धूमाद्धूमध्वजसाधने किमेतद्देशकालसंलग्नो धूमो हेतुः; किं वा अनेतद्देशकालसंलग्न इति विकल्प्य, आद्ये साधनशून्यं निदर्शनम्, द्वितीयेऽसिद्धिरिति दूषणसम्भवादिति।

१५५. मैवम्; तत्र धूममात्रस्य पर्वतेऽग्निसाधकत्वेनादूषणत्वाभ्युपगमात्।

१५६. तर्हि किं वक्रो धूमो हेतुरिति विकल्पेन दूषणप्रसङ्ग इति चेन्न; तस्य सामान्यस्यैव हेतुत्वात्।

there is the contingence of the non-existence of all inferences (as such).

154. It is as follows: in the inference of the smoke-bannered (fire) from smoke, is it the smoke that is related to this place and time, that is the probans or the smoke that is related not to the present place and time? Through such analysis, there is the contingence of defect (in the inference) as, in the first case, there is the non-existence of the probans in the example, and in the second case, there is non-establishment (of the probans in respect of the subject).

155. It is not so (says the siddhātin); for since there the smoke as such alone is what is instrumental in establishing the fire in the mountain, there is the acceptance of non-defectiveness (of the inference).

156. If it be said that in that case, through an analysis in the form "is the probans the curved smoke (or the straight one)?" there is the contingence of the defect, not so (says the siddhāntin); because it is only that (smoke) in general which is the probans.

१५७. न चास्तु तथा प्रकृतेऽपीति वाच्यम् । प्रमाणभ्रान्तिदृश्ययोः दृश्यत्वसामान्याभावात् । न हि जलनभोनलिनयोर्नलिनत्वसामान्यमस्ति ।

१५८. तर्हि कथं भ्रान्तिदृश्यत्वमित्युच्यते इति चेन्न ; यथा नभोनलिनमित्युच्यते तथैवेत्यवेहि ।

१५९. दृश्यत्वस्य सन्मात्रवृत्तित्वाद्विरुद्धता च । न च शुक्तिरजतं दृश्यमिति वाच्यम् । तत्र शुक्तिकाया एव दृश्यत्वात् ।

१६०. ननु रजतसंविदः कथं शुक्तिका विषययो विरोधादिति चेन्न ।

157. Nor may it be said "let it be likewise in the present context too", because, there is not the generality of cognisability in the validly and the delusively cognised. There is indeed no generality "lotusness" in the water-lotus and the sky-lotus.

158. If it be asked how there is the verbal usage "delusive cognisability," no (says the siddhāntin). Just as there is the verbal usage (in respect of) sky-lotus, know it to be even so (here).

159. Besides, there is the defect "being the contradictory (probans)" because cognisability is present only in the real. Nor may it be said that shell-silver is cognisable, because there cognisability belongs to shell alone.

160. "How can shell be the content of the silver-cognition since this is contradictory?" If this be said, no (says the siddhāntin).

१६१. रजतसंविदं इति कोऽर्थः? किं रजतविषयाया इति? रजतत्वोल्लेखिसंविद इति वा?

१६२. नाद्यः; अनभ्युपगमात्। द्वितीये को विरोधः? स्वविषय-शुक्तिकामेवान्याकारेण गृह्णातीत्यस्याविरुद्धत्वात्।

१६३. ननु तर्ह्यपि रजतेऽस्ति कथञ्चिद्दृश्यतेति चेन्न; तस्य दृश्यत्वाभासत्वात्। तादृशस्य पक्षेऽनन्वयात्।

१६४. किञ्च रजतस्य फलव्याप्यतया वृत्तिव्याप्यतया वा दृश्यत्वम्? नोभयमपि, अध्यस्ततयैव तत्सिध्यभ्युपगमात्। न च तत्प्रतीतावुपायान्तरं वास्ति, सन्निकर्षाभावात्। आत्मनोऽपि दृश्यत्वादनैकान्तिकता च।

161. What is the meaning "of silver cognition"? Is it "of (the cognition) which has silver for its content" or, is it "of the cognition which comprehends silver-ness?"

162. Not the first, because it is not accepted. In the second case, what is the contradiction? For, its own content, namely, shell itself it cognises in a different form—in this there is no contradiction.

163. Now, if it be contended that even then there is somehow cognisability in silver, no (says the siddhāntin), since that is a mere semblance of cognisability and since that kind (of cognisability) is not related to the subject.

164. Again, is the cognisability of the silver as pervaded by the fruit, or by the psychosis? Not even both, since its establishment is admitted to be only as super-imposed. Nor is there any other means for the cognition of that, since there is no (sense) contact.

१६५. नात्मा दृश्यते इति चेन्न; व्याहतेः। न ह्यज्ञाते धर्मिणि धर्मविधानं तन्निषेधो वा युज्यते।

१६६. आत्मा दृश्यः, वस्तुत्वात्, घटवत्। अयं घटः एतद्घटात्मान्यान्यदृश्यान्यः, प्रमेयत्वात्, घटवदिति च तस्य दृश्यत्वसिद्धेः।

१६७. किञ्च दृश्यत्वाभावे तदविद्यानिवृत्त्यभावेन मोक्षाभावप्रसङ्गः।

१६८. न च त्वत्पक्षे ब्रह्मज्ञानं नाम यत्किञ्चित्स्यात्, षष्ठ्यर्थस्य विषयतानतिरेकात्।

There is also non-conclusiveness (of the probans), because the self too is cognisable.

165. If it be said that the self is not cognised, not so (says the siddhāntin) because of self-contradiction. Indeed in respect of a non-cognised substrate, it does not stand to reason either to predicate an attribute or negate it.

166. For, its cognisability is established thus: "The self is cognisable, because it is a thing, like the pot." And, "This pot is different from that cognisable (*viz.*, self) which is different from that (world) which is other than the said pot and the self; because it is an object of knowledge, like the pot."

167. Further, since in the non-existence of cognisability (in respect of the self) there is non-existence of the destruction of nescience in respect of that, there is the contingence of the non-existence of release.

168. Nor in your system can there be something called Brahman-knowledge (which is other than knowledge with the self as the content), since the meaning

१६९. यद्धि श्रुतमयेन ज्ञानेन तत्त्वमभिप्राय चिन्तामयीमवस्था-मवलम्बमानस्यान्तःकरणपरिणामवृत्तिरूपं ज्ञानमुपजायते ; तेन भवेदविद्या-निवृत्तिरिति चेन्न ।

१७०. तथाभ्युपगमे परमात्मनोऽपि दृश्यतया व्यभिचारानिस्तारात् ।

१७१. आत्मनोऽपि वृत्तिव्याप्यत्वेऽपि फलव्याप्यताया अभावान्न दृश्यत्वमिति चेन्न ; दत्तोत्तरत्वात् ।

१७२. विषयत्वाभावेऽप्यात्माकारज्ञानमात्मज्ञानम् । तेन भवेद-विद्यानिवृत्तिरिति चेन्न ।

of the genitive is not other than "being the content (of cognition)."

169. "For him who through the knowledge gained by hearing (the scripture) understands reality and attains to the state of meditation, there arises cognition in the form of a modification of the internal organ; through that (cognition) there may be removal of nescience." If this be said, no (says the siddhāntin).

170. For, if it be so accepted there is no getting over the (defect of) inconstancy (of the probans), because of the supreme self (Paramātman) too being cognisable.

171. "Because for the self too, though there is pervadedness by psychosis there is the non-existence of pervadedness by the fruit (of cognition), there is no cognisability"; if this be said, no (says the siddhāntin), since the answer has been (already) given.

172. "Though there is non-existence of contentness, the knowledge having the form of the self is

१७३. विचारागोचरत्वात् । तथाहि—'आत्माकारमिति कोऽर्थः ? आत्माकार एवाकारो यस्येति वा ? आत्माकार इवाकारो यस्येति वा ? आत्मा आकारो यस्येति वा ?

१७४. नाद्यः ; ज्ञानज्ञेययोरेकाकारतानुपलम्भात ।

१७५. एकैव सत्ता ज्ञानज्ञेययोराकारोऽस्तीति चेन्न ; अनुगतसत्ताया अनङ्गीकारात् ।

१७६. सत्तयैकाकारत्वे च वेदान्तवाक्यजनितज्ञानमात्माकारमेव

self-knowledge; by that there may be removal of nescience." If this be said, no (says the siddhāntin).

173. Because it is beyond (the comprehension of) inquiry. It is as follows; what is the meaning (of the term) "having the form of the self?" Is it "whose form is the same as the form of the self?" Or is it "whose form is similar to the form of the self?" Or is it "which has the self for its form."

174. Not the first, because the cognition and the cognised are not perceived to have one (and the same) form.

175. If it be said that one (and the same) reality is the form for both cognition and cognised, no (says the siddhāntin) because a uniform reality (sattā) is not accepted.

176. And if there be one (and the same) form through (the same) reality (sattā), why should the knowledge resulting from the Vedāntic statements have the form of the self at all? Why should it not have the

कुतः ? घटाकारमपि किं न स्यात् । न च परेणात्मनि सत्ता नामाकारोऽङ्गीक्रियते, निराकारताङ्गीकारात् ।

१७७. न द्वितीयः ; अत्यन्तसादृश्यस्यानुपलम्भात् । किञ्चित्सादृश्यस्य प्रागिवातिप्रसञ्जकत्वात् ।

१७८. तृतीयेऽपि पक्षे नात्मा साक्षाज्ज्ञानस्याकारः सम्भवति, आधाराधेयभावस्यासम्भवात् ।

१७९. अतः परिशेषाद्विषयतया व्यावर्तकत्वेन चात्मज्ञानस्याकार इवेति वक्तव्यम् । तदेव च विषयत्वमिति यत्किञ्चिदेतत् ।

१८०. ननु भवेदिदं यदि दृग्विषयत्वं दृश्यत्वम् ; स्वप्रतिबद्ध-

form of a pot also? Nor do the others (Advaitins) admit a form called reality (sattā) in the self, because formlessness is admitted.

177. Not the second, because complete similarity is not cognised, while some kind of similarity will result in undue extension as in the prior case.

178. In the third alternative too, the self cannot directly become the form of the cognition, because of the impossibility of the relation of the container and the contained (as between cognition and the self).

179. Therefore by elimination, it should be said that as the content and as what excludes, the self is the form, as it were, of cognition; and since this itself is contentness, this (objection) is a trifle.

XIX

180. "Now, if cognisability is to be the object of cognition there would be this (group of defects). The

व्यवहारे स्वातिरिक्तसंविदपेक्षानियतिर्दृश्यत्वम्'। कथमेतादृशी दृश्यता कथितदूषणगणग्रस्ता स्यात्?

१८१. मैवम्; अतिरिक्तपदेन पारमार्थिकभेदवत्त्वं वा आविद्यक-भेदवत्त्वं वा?

१८२. नाद्यः; तवासिद्धेः। न द्वितीयः; ममासिद्धेः।

१८३. सामान्यतः प्रयोग इति च प्रागेव परास्तम्। संविदपेक्षा-नियतत्वमात्रस्य हेतुत्वोपपत्तेर्व्यर्थविशेषणत्वञ्च।

१८४. न चास्ति रजतेऽपि ज्ञानापेक्षा व्यवहाराय तस्याध्यस्तत-यैव सिध्यभ्युपगमादित्यवादिष्म।

invariable dependence on a cognition other than itself in respect of the empirical usage related to some thing, is cognisability. How can cognisability of this kind be tainted by the group of defects adduced"?

181. Not so (says the siddhāntin). By the words "other than" (what is it that is meant)—having real difference, or having the difference resulting from nescience?

182. Not the first, because it is not established for you (the Advaitin). Not the second, because it is not established for me (the Dvaitin).

183. And that the usage is (in respect of difference) in general, this has (already) been refuted. And the invariability of dependence on a cognition being itself intelligible as the probans, the qualification (other than itself) is futile.

184. And even in respect of silver there is no dependence on (another) cognition for the sake of

१८५. अत्यन्तासत्यनैकान्त्यश्च ।

१८६. न च तदपि मिथ्येति वाच्यम् । तथा सति रजतादेरसद्विलक्षणत्वप्रतिपादनप्रयासवैयर्थ्यापातात् ।

१८७. न च बाध्यत्वमसतो युज्यते, अप्रतीत्यङ्गीकारात् । नापि तस्यानिर्वचनीयत्वम् , तस्य प्रमाणाभावादिति ।

१८८. न च जडत्वहेतुरपि निगदितदूषणगणलङ्घने जङ्घालः । तथाहि—किमिदं जडत्वं नाम ? ज्ञानानाधारत्वं वा ? अनात्मत्वं वा ? अज्ञानरूपत्वं वा ? अस्वप्रकाशत्वं वा ?

empirical usage, since its establishment is admitted only as superimposed (merely phenomenal, thus requiring neither a psychosis of manas nor intelligence as reflected in that psychosis): this we have said.

185. There is also non-conclusiveness (of the probans) in respect of the absolutely unreal.

186. Nor can it be said that that too is illusory; for, in that case there is the contingence of futility of the effort to predicate the difference from the unreal in respect of silver, etc.

187. Nor does sublatability stand to reason in the case of the unreal, since its non-cognition is accepted. Nor can there be indeterminability for it, because there is no authority for it (*i.e.*, indeterminability).

XX

188. The probans "inertness" too has not the legs (strong enough) to jump over the adduced group of defects. It is as follows: what is the meaning of this

१८९. नाद्यः; विशिष्टात्मनि पक्षनिक्षिप्तेऽसिद्धत्वात्। असदात्मनोर्विपक्षभूतयोश्च वर्तमानत्वात्।

१९०. न द्वितीयः, अनात्मत्वपदेन—आत्मातिरिक्तत्वं वा आत्मत्वानाधारत्वं वा विवक्षितम्?

१९१. नाद्यः; तवासिद्धेः। न हि त्वत्पक्षे परमात्मनो जगदतिरिक्तमस्ति।

१९२. परमार्थतस्तदभावेऽप्यनाद्यविद्याविलसितो भेदोऽस्तीति चेत्—तर्ह्यस्माकमसिद्धो हेतुः। असति व्यभिचारश्च।

that is called inertness? Is it (1) not being a substrate of cognition, (2) or not being the self (non-self-hood) or (3) being the form of nescience, (4) or not being self-luminous?

189. Not the first, because there is (partial) non-establishment (of the probans in the subject), in respect of the qualified self included in the subject, (and) because it (the probans) is present in the absolutely unreal and the self which form the negative instances.

190. Not the second. What is it that is intended by the term "not being the self (Anātman)"? (1) Is it being other than the self or (2) not being a substrate of self-hood (Ātmatva).

191. Not the first, because it is not established for you (the Advaitin). Indeed according to your (the Advaitin's) school there is no world as other than the supreme self (Paramātman).

192. "Though there is the non-existence of that (difference) as (absolutely) real, there is the difference

१९३. न द्वितीयः; आत्मत्वस्य प्रागुक्तप्रकारान्तर्भावे साध्याविशिष्टतासिध्यनैकान्त्यान्यतमापातात् ।

१९४. एतेन यत् त्वयात्मत्वमभिप्रेतम्, तदेवास्त्वस्माकमिति परिहृतम् । अस्माकमुक्तप्रकारान्यतमसङ्ग्रहसम्भवात् ।

१९५. न तृतीयः; वृत्तिज्ञानभागेऽसिद्धत्वात् । आत्मनो ज्ञानस्वरूपता न निर्बाधतामारोहति । तथाहि—तज्ज्ञानं सविषयं निर्विषयं वा ?

as manifested by beginningless nescience"; if this be said, the probans is not established for us (the Dvaitins) (since nescience-produced-difference is not admitted by us). And there is the inconstancy (of the probans) in respect of the (absolutely) unreal (since you admit the unreal to be illusory).

193. Not the second; for if self-hood be brought under the alternatives stated already, there is the contingence of one of (the three defects), non-distinction from probandum, non-establishment (of the probans), and non-conclusiveness (of the probans).

194. By this, (the argument) "the self-hood understood by you (Dvaitins), let that be the same for us (Advaitins)" is also refuted, because for us (the Dvaitins) it is possible to adopt any one of the alternatives stated.

195. Not the third, for there is non-establishment (of the probans) in respect of that part (of the subject) which is cognitive psychosis. The position that the self is of the nature of knowledge does not come up to the

१९६. आद्ये स्वविषयं परविषयं वा ? नाद्यः; स्ववृत्तिविरोधात् । न द्वितीयः; मोक्षे ज्ञानाभावप्रसङ्गात् । नोत्तरः; ज्ञानत्वस्यैवाभावप्रसङ्गात् ।

१९७. निर्विषयज्ञानरूपत्वे चास्तु प्रपञ्चेऽपि तादृशज्ञानरूपत्वमित्यसिद्धिप्रसङ्गः ।

१९८. न चतुर्थः; स्वकर्मकसंविद्रूपतामन्तरेण स्वप्रकाशान्तरस्योत्तरत्र वारयिष्यमाणत्वात् । स्वकर्मकप्रकाशत्वस्यात्मन्यपि तवाभावादिति ।

(level of) being tenable. It is as follows; has that knowledge a content or has it no content?

196. In the first case, has it itself as content or another as content? Not the first, because of contradiction of functioning in respect of itself. Not the second, because of the contingence of the non-existence of knowledge in release. Not the latter (not having a content), because of the contingence of the non-existence of the very nature of knowledge.

197. And if it is to be of the form of contentless cognition, let there be such a form for cognition in the world too; thus there is the contingence of the non-establishment (of the probans, inertness).

198. Not the fourth. For, (the definition of) any other self-luminosity as distinct from "that form of cognition which has itself for object" will be refuted later on, while according to you (the Advaitin) the luminosity which has itself for object is non-existent even in the self.

१९९. एतेनाचेतनत्वं जडत्वमिति निरस्तम् । उक्तपक्षाबहिर्भावात् ।

२००. अस्माभिर्ज्ञातृत्वानाधारत्वस्य जडत्वेनाभिलापान्नास्मत्प्रतिबन्दी ।

२०१. परिच्छिन्नहेतुरपि न साध्यसाधकतामध्यास्ते । तथा हि—परिच्छिन्नत्वं नाम देशतः परिच्छिन्नत्वं वा? कालतो वा? अन्योन्याभावाधिकरणत्वं वा?

२०२. नाद्यः; कालाकाशादिभागेऽसिद्धेः ।

199. By this (the view) that inertness is non-sentience is also refuted, because it does not fall outside the alternatives already mentioned.

200. Nor can there be the adoption (of a position) similar to ours (by the Advaitins) since "not being the substrate of knowership" is called inertness by us (and that is not acceptable to the Advaitin).

XXI

201. The probans "finitude" too cannot stand as what can establish the probandum. It is as follows: what is it that is meant by the term "finitude"? Is it spatial finitude or temporal finitude, or being the substrate of reciprocal non-existence?

202. Not the first, for there is partial non-establishment (of the probans) in respect of time (*i.e.*, *aṁśikāla*) and ether (not *bhūtākāśa*).

२०३. अत एव न द्वितीयः; ब्रह्मव्यतिरिक्तं सकलमपि देशकालाभ्यां परिच्छिन्नमिति चेन्न; व्याघातात्।

२०४. तथाहि—देशतः परिच्छिन्नत्वं नाम कचिन्निष्ठाभावप्रतियोगिता। तथा च सर्वस्याभावं प्रतिजानता किञ्चिदधिष्ठानमभ्युपेयम्। अभावस्याधिष्ठानबोधाधीनबोधत्वात्। तथा च कथं न व्याघातः?

२०५. सकलमपि ब्रह्मण्यध्यस्तम्। अतस्तत्र नास्तीति निषेधाश्चाधिष्ठानाभ्युपगत्या व्याघात इति चेन्न; परिच्छिन्नता नाम बाध्यतेत्यर्थः स्यात्। तथात्वे साध्याविशिष्टतयैव दुष्टतापत्तिः।

203. For the same reason it is not the second. If it be said that everything other than Brahman has spatial and temporal finitude, no, because of contradiction.

204. It is as follows: to be finite in space is to be the counter-correlate of the (absolute) non-existence located in some place. And thus by him who premises the non-existence of everything, some substrate has to be accepted; for, of the non-existence the cognition is dependent on the cognition of the substrate; and thus how can there be no contradiction?

205. If it be said that everything (in the world) is superimposed on Brahman, and that therefore there is no contradiction because of the acceptance of the substrate through the denial in the form, "there it is not," no, (says the siddhāntin). (For) the meaning would be that what is called finitude is sublatability; if that would be so, there is the contingence of the

२०६. कालपरिच्छेदे चानित्यता सादिता त्रिकालसत्यता वाभिप्रेता भवेत् । तथा च कालस्यैतादृशपरिच्छेदायोगेनागतः स एव दुरात्मा व्याघातः ।

२०७. कुतश्चाकाशादेः कालपरिच्छेदाध्यवसायः? जडत्वहेतुनेति चेन्न; तस्यापाकृतत्वात्, घटादौ कार्यताप्रयुक्तत्वाच्च परिच्छिन्नत्वस्य ।

२०८. यज्जडं तत्कार्यमिति चेन्न; अविद्यायां व्यभिचारात् । तस्याश्च कार्यत्वेऽनादित्वपरिभाषा परिलुप्येत । तत्कारणस्याभावश्च ।

defect, even because of non-distinction from the probandum.

206. And by temporal finitude might be intended "being non-eternal" or "having a beginning" or "not being real in all three times (the past, future and the present)"; and thus, because of the impossibility of such a finitude in respect of time, that same contradiction of vile nature has come (again).

207. By what (authority) do we determine temporal finitude in respect of ether? If it be said (that it is) by the probans, inertness, it is not so (says the siddhāntin) because it has been refuted, also because the finitude in the case of pot, etc., is brought about by (the adjunct) "being an effect".

208. If it be said that whatever is inert is an effect, it is not so (says the siddhāntin), because of inconstancy in respect of nescience. And if that be an effect, there would be the failure of the technical exposition in respect of that (nescience) as beginningless; and there is non-existence of a cause for it.

२०९. पञ्चमप्रकारं मोक्षमाचक्षाणस्य· जडत्वहेतोर्मोक्षे नित्यतयाभ्युपगते व्यभिचारः।

२१०. तस्य च कालपरिच्छिन्नत्वे पुनरावृत्तिप्रसङ्गः। न हि सहस्राक्षोऽपि क्षयं क्षेप्तुं क्षम इत्युन्मत्तवादश्च स्यात्।

२११. न तृतीयः; "नेति नेति" इत्यादिना ब्रह्मण्यपि जगदन्योन्याभावाधिकरणतायाः श्रुतत्वात्। सोऽपि भेदोऽविद्याविलसित इति चेन्न।

२१२. तत्किमिदानीं परमार्थभेदभिन्नत्वं हेतुः? तथा सति पक्षे तदसिद्धिः स्यात्, विरुद्धता च स्यादिति। सन् घट इत्यादिप्रत्यक्षेण बाधितविषयत्वात् कालात्ययापदिष्टश्च।

209. There is the inconstancy of the probans "inertness", if accepted as eternal, in respect of release, for him who speaks of release as of a fifth form.

210. And if that (release—mokṣa) has temporal finitude, there is the contingence of the return (to the world of saṁsāra). Not even the thousand eyed (Indra) has the capacity to annul destruction; hence (your position) would be the raving of a lunatic.

XXII

211. Not the third. Scriptural statements like "not this" "not this" declare that Brahman is the substrate of the reciprocal non-existence of the world. If that difference too be declared a product of nescience, (it is) not so (says the siddhantin).

212. Then is here "being different because of real difference" the probans? In that case there would be the non-establishment of that in the subject, and

२१३. ननु केयं सत्यता या प्रत्यक्षगोचरा? किं सत्त्वं वा? विधिगम्यत्वं वा? अर्थक्रियाकारित्वं वा? प्रातिभासिकेतरत्वं वा? असत्वातिरिक्तत्वं वा? अबाध्यत्वं वा?

२१४. आद्यपञ्चकान्यतमाभ्युपगमेनास्माकं प्रत्यक्षाविरोधः, तस्यास्माभिरनिराकरणात् ।

२१५. न षष्ठः; प्रत्यक्षस्योत्तरकालीनबाधाभावग्राहितायोगात् । तस्मात्सद्गन्धर्वनगरमित्यादिवदयं प्रत्यक्षेण सत्त्वग्रहणप्रवाद इति ।

there would also be contradiction. And since by perceptions like, "the pot is real" there is sublation of the content (of the inference), (the probans) becomes adduced after the lapse of the (proper) time (*i.e.*, becomes sublated).

213. Now, what is this "being real" which is the sphere of perception? (1) Is it reality or (2) being made known by an affirmation or (3) producing succesful activity (in respect of the object) or (4) being other than merely apparent or (5) being other than non-reality or (6) non-sublatability?

214. On the acceptance of any one of the first five (alternatives) there is not for us (Advaitins) conflict with perception, because that (kind of reality) is not rejected by us (Advaitins).

215. Not the sixth, because it is not possible for perception to apprehend the non-existence of sublation subsequently. Therefore, this contention that reality is apprehended by perception is like (the assertion) "the city of Gandharvas is real".

२१६. मैवम्; अबाध्यतायाः प्रत्यक्षग्राह्यत्वात्। न च तस्योत्तरकालीनबाधाभावाग्राहकत्वमिति वाच्यम्। तदानीमबाध्यताग्रहणेनैव

२१७. तत्कालीनाबाध्यता गन्धर्वनगरेऽपि गृह्यते इति चेत्; सत्यम्; तथाप्यस्ति विशेषः। प्रामाण्यं हि ज्ञानस्योत्सर्गतोऽपवादादप्रामाण्यमिति विद्वत्सम्मतिः।

२१८. तथा च तत्र बाधकादप्रामाण्यमुपस्थाप्यते। प्रकृते तु तादृशबाधकादर्शनात् त्रिकालाबाध्यतैव निरपवादा सिध्यतीति।

216. (If the Advaitins advance this argument) it is not so (says the siddhāntin), since non-sublation is perceptually apprehended. Nor may it be said that it (perception) does not apprehend non-existence of sublation subsequently; for this is established even by the apprehension of non-sublatedness at that time.

217. "Non-sublatedness at that time is apprehended even of the city of Gandharvas"; if this be said, true. Even then there is a difference. "Validity of cognition is, indeed, the general rule; invalidity is because of defect;" this is what is accepted by the learned.

218. And thus, there, invalidity is brought in through some sublater; in the case in question, since that kind of sublation is not seen, it is only non-sublatability in all three times that is established, free from defect.

२१९. अस्त्वनुमानमेव बाधकं प्रत्यक्षस्येति चेन्न; प्रत्यक्षविरोधेन प्राप्तमरणावस्थस्य प्रत्यक्षविरोधाक्षमत्वात्। अन्यथा दहनशैत्यानुमानमपि तदुष्णतावगाहिप्रत्यक्षबाधकत्वेन प्रमाणं प्रसज्येत। यदा च प्रत्यक्षं समबलप्रत्यक्षान्तरेण न बाध्यते, हन्त! तदा का वार्ता तत्पादोपजीविनो वराकस्य तर्कस्य तद्बाधकत्वे।

२२०. नभोमलिनतामाकलयत्प्रत्यक्षममूर्तानुमानेन बाधितं दृष्टमिति चेन्न; तत्राप्याप्तवाक्यादिनैव बाधाभ्युपगमेनासम्प्रतिपत्तेः।

XXIII

219. If it be said, "Let inference itself be the sublater of perception," no; for, (the inference) reduced to the death-state by the contradiction with perception, is incapable of contradicting the perception. Otherwise, even the inference of the coldness of fire would become valid as the sublater of the perception comprehending heat (in fire). And when perception is not sublated by another perception of equal strength, what then, alas! is the talk about the wretch, namely, reasoning which lives at the feet of that (perception), being the sublater of that?

220. If it be said that the perception that apprehends the sky as sullied (by smoke etc.,) is seen to be sublated by the inference of its being incorporeal, no (says the siddhāntin); for, even there, since the acceptance of the sublation is solely due to the testimony of reliable persons, etc., there is no admission (of sublation by inference).

२२१. यदा च पुनः स्वयमेवानुमिमीते, तदापि बलवत्प्रत्यक्षगृहीतव्याप्तिकादेव तस्मादध्यवसायः ।

२२२. प्रत्यक्षत्वाद्गन्धर्वनगरप्रत्यक्षवद्विप्रतिपन्नमपि प्रत्यक्षं भ्रान्तं किं न स्यादिति चेन्न। तर्हि वाक्यत्वाज्जरद्गवादिवाक्यवत्सत्यज्ञानादिवाक्यमप्रमाणं किं न स्यात्?

२२३. किञ्च प्रत्यक्षशब्देन प्रत्यक्षाभासविवक्षायां पक्षे तदभावः ।

२२४. प्रमाणाभिप्राये दृष्टान्ते ऽनन्वयः । ज्ञानत्वमात्रस्य हेतुत्वे सत्यज्ञानादिवचनजन्यज्ञाने व्यभिचारः ।

221. And again even when there is inference by one's own self, then too there is ascertainment from that (inference) only as possessing a pervasion apprehended by a perception which is strong (as compared with the inference).

222. If it be asked, "why should not then the perception which is under dispute also be delusive, because it is a perception like the perception of the city of the Gandharvas?" no. Then why should not statements like "existence, knowledge, etc.", be invalid, because they are statements, like the statements about the aged ox?

223. Further if by the term "perception" be intended the semblance of perception, it is non-existent in the subject.

224. If a means of valid knowledge be intended, it is not related to the example. If "merely being knowledge" be the probans, there is the inconstancy

२२५. विश्वं सत्यमित्याद्यागमविरोधश्च । व्यावहारिकं सत्त्वमत्रोच्यते इति चेन्न ; निर्बीजत्वात्कल्पनायाः ।

२२६. व्यर्थं च प्रपञ्चे व्यावहारिकसत्यत्वप्रतिपादनम् । न हि कश्चिल्लौकिको वैदिको वा व्यावहारिकसत्यतां प्रपञ्चे नाभ्युपैति ।

२२७. तस्माद्वादिप्रसिद्धमिथ्यात्वनिषेधेन पारमार्थिकसत्त्वमेव प्रतिपाद्यते, "अप्राप्ते शास्त्रमर्थवत्" इति न्यायात् ।

२२८. "नेह नाना" इत्यादिश्रुतिनिषेध्यसमर्पकतयानुवदति

(of the probans) in respect of the knowledge given rise to by statements like "existence, knowledge, etc."

XXIV

225. Besides, there is contradiction with scriptural statements like "the world is real", etc. If it be said that phenomenal reality (alone) is predicated here, no (says the siddhāntin), because the assumption is groundless.

226. And it is futile to predicate phenomenal reality with reference to the world. Nobody, whether worldly (wise) or (learned) in the vedas, fails to accept the phenomenal reality of the world.

227. Therefore there is predicated only noumenal reality through the refutation of illusoriness well-known to the opponent (the Advaitin), because of the principle that scripture is purportful with reference to what is not established (otherwise).

228. If it be said that the statement of the reality of the universe is a repetition (of what is otherwise

विश्वसत्यतावाक्यमिति चेन्न; तथा सति विश्वं सत्यमित्यादिवचनविधान-सिद्ध्यर्थं "नेह नाना" इत्यनुवाद इति प्रसङ्गात्।

२२९. किञ्च "असदेवेदमग्र आसीत्" इत्यादिवाक्यनिषेध्य-समर्पकतया सत्यज्ञानादिवाक्यं ब्रह्मणः सत्यतामनुवदतीति चातिप्रसङ्गः।

२३०. विश्वमिथ्यात्वब्रह्मसत्यत्वे श्रुतिमन्तरा न सिद्ध्यत इति कथमनुवाद इति चेन्न; दृश्यत्वादिहेतुना मिथ्यात्वसाधनात्। भ्रमानुप-पत्त्याधिष्ठानतया ब्रह्मणोऽपि सत्यत्वकल्पनात्।

established) in order to make known what is negated by the scriptural statements like "there are no differents whatsoever here" no (says the siddhāntin); for, in that case, there is the contingence that in order to secure the affirmation in such texts as "the world is real", the statement "there are no differents whatsoever here" is a repetition.

229. Further, there is the undue extension, that in order to make known what is negated by sentences like "this was only non-existence at the beginning" the text "reality, knowledge, etc." is a restatement of Brahman's reality.

230. "When the illusoriness of the universe and the reality of Brahman cannot be established by (any means) other than scripture how can there be a restatement (of them)?" If this be asked, no (says the siddhāntin), because by probans like cognisability, there is establishment of illusoriness, and because, through the unintelligibility of delusion (otherwise), there is the assumption in the case of Brahman too that as substrate it is real.

२३१. किञ्च विश्वसत्यत्वानुवाद इति वदता विश्वस्य प्रामाणिकताभ्युपेयते ? न वा ?

२३२. नाद्यः; तत्प्रमाणाविरोधात् । निषेध्यस्य स्वेन प्रमाणाविषयतानभ्युपगमाच्च ।

२३३. न द्वितीयः; असिद्धस्यानुवादायोगात् । लोकसिद्धानुवाद इति चेन्न; लोके च प्रमाणसिद्धमनूद्यते ? भ्रान्त्या वा ?

२३४. नाद्यः, दत्तोत्तरत्वात्; नोत्तरः, तथैव लोकस्य भ्रान्तिसिद्धब्रह्मसद्भावो निषिद्ध्यते इति प्रसङ्गात् ।

231. Further, by him who says that there is repetition of the reality of the world, is the world admitted as an object of valid cognition or not ?

232. Not the first, because of conflict with that authority (for statements like " There are no differents " etc.), and because of the fact that that which is negated is not admitted (by you Advaitin) to be by its own nature the content of valid cognition.

233. Not the second, because restatement of that which is not established is impossible. If it be said that there is restatement of what is established in ordinary experience, no (says the siddhāntin). Is it the restatement of what is established on valid evidence in ordinary experience or delusively ?

234. Not the first, because of the reply having been already given. Not the latter, because in the same way there is the contingence of the refutation of Brahman-reality delusively cognised in the case of the world.

२३५. तस्माद्यद्वदन्तीत्यादिवचनं परिहारे विशेषयुक्तिं च विनानुवादायोगात् । व्यावहारिकसत्यत्वस्य च वक्तुमप्रयोजकत्वात् । पारमार्थिकमेव सत्यत्वं जगत्युदितमित्यस्ति श्रुतिविरोधः ।

२३६. "असत्यमप्रतिष्ठं ते जगदाहुरनीश्वरम्" इति निरवकाशस्मृतिविरोधश्च ।

२३७. न चात्रासत्यशब्दोऽत्यन्तासत्यपरः; अत्यन्तासत्त्वाभ्युपगन्तुर्वादिन एवाभावादाहुरित्यस्यायोगादिति ।

235. Therefore, there is no possibility of repetitiveness in the absence of a statement like "what they say" and a special argument for the refutation; and there is no ground for predicating phenomenal reality (alone). For these reasons, it is absolute reality that is declared of the world; hence there is the conflict with scripture (for the Advaitin's inference).

XXV

236. Besides there is the conflict (for the Advaitin's position) with the code (smṛti) devoid of room (for ambigivuity) namely, "They say that the universe is non-real, has no substrate, and has no Lord. (What is there that does not spring from mutual union? Lust is the cause of all)".

237. And here the word "not-real" has not for purport absolute unreality; for, because of the non-existence of any disputant who accepts absolute unreality, (the term) "they say" would not be possible.

२३८. विप्रतिपन्नं सत्यं प्रमाणादृष्टत्वात्, ब्रह्मवत्, इत्यनुमान-विरोधश्च ।

२३९. न च साध्यानिरूक्तिः; अबाध्यतायाः साध्यत्वात् । तस्याश्च ब्रह्मणि सिद्धत्वान्नाप्रसिद्धविशेषणता ।

२४०. ननु किमिदं प्रमाणदृष्टत्वम्? तात्त्विकप्रमाणदृष्टत्वम्? अतात्त्विकप्रमाणदृष्टत्वं वा?

२४१. नाद्यः; अस्माकमसिद्धेः । प्रत्यक्षादिप्रमाणानां तत्त्वा-वेदकतानभ्युपगमात् ।

XXVI

238. And there is conflict with the (following) inference: "The thing under dispute is real, because it is cognised through a means of valid knowledge, like Brahman."

239. Nor is the probandum undefined, since being non-sublatable (itself) is the probandum. And because of the establishment of that (non-sublatability) in the case of Brahman, there is not (the defect of) non-established qualification.

240. Now, what is this being cognised through a means of valid knowledge? Is it being cognised through a real means of valid knowledge, or being cognised through a non-real means of valid knowledge?

241. Not the first, because it is not established for us (the Advaitins), since means of valid knowledge like perception, etc. are not admitted as making known reality.

२४२. नोत्तरः; तवासिद्धेः। साधनविकलत्वं च दृष्टान्तस्येति।

२४३. मैवम्; प्रत्यक्षादिप्रमाणानामतत्त्वावेदकत्वे मानाभावात्। प्रत्यक्षादिकं तत्त्वावेदकं प्रमाणत्वात्, सत्यज्ञानादिवाक्यवत्। अन्यथा प्रमाणमेव न स्यात्। प्रपञ्चस्तत्त्वावेदकप्रमाणदृष्टः; सम्प्रतिपन्नभ्रान्तपदार्थेतरत्वात्; ब्रह्मवत्।

२४४. आत्मत्वमुपाधिरिति चेन्न; अबाध्यत्वादेरात्मत्वस्य पक्षे सम्भवात्। अन्यथात्मत्वस्याप्यभावस्स्याद्ब्रह्मणि।

242. Not the latter, because it is not established for you (the Dvaitins). And the example too is devoid of the Probans.

243. Not so (says the siddhāntin); for, there is no authority in respect of means of valid knowledge like perception making known (only) the non-real. Perception, etc. make known the real, because of being a means of valid knowledge, like (the text) "reality, knowledge, etc." Otherwise there would not at all be (for those) the character of being means of valid knowledge. The universe is cognised through a means of valid knowledge which makes known the real, because it is other than the admitted objects of delusive cognition, like Brahman.

244. If self-hood be said to be the adjunct (present in the example, and not in the subject), no (says the siddhāntin), because self-hood consisting of non-sublatability, etc., is possible in the subject; otherwise in Brahman there would be the non-existence of self-hood too.

२४५. किञ्च तत्त्वावेदकत्वादिविशेषानवधूय प्रमाणमात्रदृष्टत्वं हेतुः किं न स्यात्? न ह्यस्य विपक्षे वृत्तिः। वृत्तिव्याप्यताया आत्मन्यभ्युपगमान्न तत्र साधनावृत्तिः।

२४६. तथापि प्रामाणिकत्वातिरिक्तं सत्यत्वं नास्तीति साध्याविशिष्टतेति चेन्न; स्वपरासंमतेः।

२४७. न तावत्स्वरीत्येदमुक्तम्। प्रमाणाविषयस्यापि ब्रह्मणः सत्यत्वाभ्युपगमात्।

245. Besides, why should not the probans be "being cognised through a means of valid knowledge," in general, omitting attributes like "which makes known the real"? This probans is indeed not present in the negative instance. Since pervasion by (cognition) psychosis is accepted in respect of the self, there is not the non-existence of the probans in that (positive instance).

246. If it be said that even thus, since there is no reality other than being an object of a means of valid knowledge, there is (the defect of) non-distinction (of the probans) from the probandum, no (says the Dvaitin) since this is not accepted by yourselves (Advaitins) or by others (Dvaitins).

247. Now this is not stated according to your (Advaitin's) own point of view; for reality is admitted of Brahman though (it is) not the object of a means of valid knowledge.

२४८. नाप्यस्मद्रीत्या, ब्रह्मण इव प्रपञ्चस्यास्माभिः प्रामाणिकत्वातिरिक्तस्य सत्यत्वस्याभ्युपगमात्। अन्यथा शशविषाणवत् प्रमाणवृत्त्ययोगात्।

२४९. तथापि ब्रह्मणः प्रामाणिकत्वाभावात्साधनविकलो दृष्टान्त इति चेन्न; असाधारणस्य दूषणत्वाभावपक्षे केवलव्यतिरेकित्वोपपत्तेः। ब्रह्मणश्चाप्रामाणिकत्वे शशविषाणवदसत्त्वप्रसङ्गः।

२५०. स्वतः सिद्धत्वान्नेति चेन्न; स्वत इति स्वेनेति वा प्रमाणेन विनेति वा।

248. Nor is it according to our (Dvaitins') point of view; for, of the world as of Brahman, there is admitted reality other than "being an object of a means of valid knowledge". Otherwise like the horns of a hare there would be no functioning of a means of valid knowledge.

249. If it be said that even thus, the example is devoid of probans, since Brahman is not an object of a means of valid knowledge, no (says the siddhāntin); for on the view that "uncommon" (probans) is no defect at all, there is intelligibility for the barely negative (pervasion). And if Brahman be not the object of a means of valid knowledge, there is the contingence of unreality (for it), as for the horns of a hare.

250. If it be said that it is not so, because of being established by itself, no (says the siddhāntin). The term "by itself", does it mean, "by oneself or "without a means of valid knowledge?"

२५१. नाद्यः; अनभ्युपगमात्। न हि स्वस्मिन्स्वस्य कारकताभ्युपगम्यते। अन्यथा शशविषाणस्याप्येवं सिद्धिः स्यात्।

२५२. न द्वितीयः, प्रमाणाभावे सत्त्वं न स्यादित्यस्य प्रमाणेन विना सिद्ध्यतीत्यस्यानुत्तरत्वात् सिद्ध्युपायान्तरस्यानुपन्यस्तत्वात्। स्वतःसिद्धत्वं नाम स्वप्रकाशत्वमिति चेन्न; दत्तोत्तरत्वात्।

२५३. अर्थक्रियाकारित्वाच्च सत्यत्वसाधनं संभवति। स्वाप्ररंभासंभोगादौ व्यभिचार इति चेन्न; पक्षसमत्वात्। न हि पक्षे पक्षसदृशे वा व्यभिचारः।

251. Not the first, because it is not accepted. There is not indeed admitted causal correlateness for oneself in respect of oneself; otherwise there could be establishment thus even for the horns of hare.

252. Not the second; for, (to the statement) "there is no reality in the absence of a means of valid knowledge," it is no answer (to say) that it is established without a means of valid knowledge, since no other method of establishment is stated. If it be said that "self-establishment" means "self-luminosity", no (says the siddhāntin), since it has already been answered.

XXVII

253. There is also the possibility of establishment of reality because of producing successful activity (in respect of the object). If it be said that there is the inconstancy (of the probans) in respect of cases like the enjoyment of Rambhā (a celestial damsel) in dreams, no (says the siddhāntin), because that (dream

२५४. रज्जुभुजङ्गादौ व्यभिचार इति चेन्न; तज्ज्ञानस्यैव भयकम्पादिजनकत्वात् ।

२५५. ननु ज्ञानमात्रमेव भयकम्पादिजनकम्, अर्थविशेषितं वा? आद्ये सकलज्ञानानां भयकम्पादिजनकत्वप्रसङ्गः ।

२५६. द्वितीये सर्पस्यापि तज्जनकत्वमायातमिति चेन्न; सर्पतया ज्ञातरज्जोरेव विशेषणत्वेन व्यभिचाराभावात्, सर्पाजन्यत्वाच्च ।

experience) is on a par with the subject. There is indeed no inconstancy of the probans in the subject or in what is on a par with the subject.

254. If it be said that there is the inconstancy (of the probans) in respect of rope-snake, etc. (which produce fear), no (says the siddhāntin), because its cognition by itself produces fear, trembling, etc. (and that cognition is not illusory).

255. Now, is it the cognition by itself that gives rise to fear, trembling, etc., or is it as specified by the content? In the first case, there is the contingence of all cognitions giving rise to fear, trembling, etc.

256. "In the second case, for the snake too there results the production of that." If this be said, no (says the siddhāntin), because, "the (real) rope that is cognised as the snake,"—this alone being the specification, there is no inconstancy (of the probans), and because they (fear etc.) are generated not by the snake (but only by snake-cognition).

२५७. आत्मन्यर्थक्रियाकारित्वं नास्तीति चेन्न; तस्य निखिलप्रपञ्चकारणत्वेन श्रुतिशतसमधिगतत्वात्। सोऽपि पक्षनिक्षिप्तश्चेत् माहायानिकपक्षपातः स्यात्।

२५८. तदतिरिक्तात्माभ्युपगमान्नैवमिति चेन्न; तदतिरिक्तस्याप्येतद्विशेषणवत्तया पक्षनिक्षेपात्।

२५९. किञ्च विशिष्टस्याप्यात्मनोऽर्थक्रियाभ्युपगमादात्मांशस्य सा कथं न स्यात्?

२६०. व्यावहारिकत्वञ्च विश्वसत्यतायां प्रमाणम्; अभिज्ञाभिवदनादीनामपि शुक्तिमात्रविषयत्वात्।

257. If it be said that in the self there is no production of successful activity (in respect of the object), no (says siddhāntin); for, it (the self) as the cause of the entire universe is well-known from a hundred scriptural statements. If that (causal self) too be (said to be) included in the subject, then there would be partiality in favour of Mahāyāna (Buddhism).

258. If it be said that it is not so because of the acceptance of a self other than that (qualified self), no (says the siddhāntin); for, since even what is other than that has this attribute (*viz.* being other than the qualified self), it is included in the subject.

259. Besides, because of the acceptance of successful activity in respect of even the qualified self, how can it be said not to be present in the self-part (of the qualified self)?

260. And, being an object of empirical usage is the authority for (the establishment of) the reality in

२६१. दोषगम्यत्वमुपाधिश्च । न च दृश्यत्वादिना प्रपञ्चेऽपि तत्साद्ध्यम् । मिथ्यात्वसाधने इवात्रापि दोषप्रसक्तेः ॥

२६२. अनिर्वचनीयत्वाविद्यातत्कार्ययोरन्यतरत्वस्य मिथ्यात्वाभिप्राये निदर्शनस्य साध्यविकलत्वं च ।

२६३. ननु कादाचित्कत्वहेतुना सकारणकत्वानुमाने कारणस्य सदसद्रूपत्वासंभवादविद्याकार्यत्वमेव पर्यवस्यतीति चेन्न ।

respect of the universe; for, even in respect of cognition, verbal designation, etc. the shell alone is the content.

XXVIII

261. And, "being the content of a cognition generated by defect" is the adjunct. Nor can that (adjunct) be established in respect of the universe too by (the probans) cognisability, etc.; for, there is the contingence of the defect here too, as in the establishment of illusoriness.

XXIX

262. And if illusoriness means indeterminability or either being nescience or being a product thereof, there is (the defect of) the non-existence of the probandum in the example.

263. "Now, in inferring possession of a cause through the probans, 'being occasional,' since it is not possible for the cause to be of the form of real and unreal, there remains only production by nescience;" if this be said, no (says the siddhāntin).

२६४. केयं कादाचित्कता नाम ? कदाचित्प्रतीतता वा ? कदाचिदुत्पन्नता वा ?

२६५. नाद्यः; व्याप्त्यभावात्। नोत्तरः; हेतोरसिद्धत्वात्। तस्मान्न त्रिविधोऽप्ययं प्रयोगो युक्तिपथमवतरतीति।

२६६. किञ्च—यदि जगद्भ्रांतिकल्पितं स्यात्, तर्हि कल्प्यमानजगत्सदृशसत्याधिष्ठानप्रधानपूर्वकमङ्गीकार्थं प्रसज्येत।

२६७. न च सत्यजगद्द्वयाङ्गीकारो युक्तः पिण्याकयाचनार्थं गतस्य खारीतैलप्रदानप्रतिज्ञावदधिकापातात।

264. What is it that is called "being occasional"? Is it being cognised on some occasion or is it being produced on some occasion?

265. Not the first, since there is no pervasion. Not the latter, because the probans is not established. Hence, this syllogism does not in any one of these three forms come into line with reason.

XXX

266. Further, if the universe be delusively posited then there would be the contingence of having to admit the antecedence of a substrate and achetype that are real and similar to the universe (so) posited.

267. And the admission of two real universes does not stand to reason, because of the contingence of excess, as in the case of him who went to beg for oil-cake and was promised a measure of oil.

२६८. ततो नेदं जगद्भ्रांतिकल्पितमिति तर्कपराहतं दृश्यत्वानुमानम् ।

२६९. किञ्च कल्पनाया आरोप्यसदृशाधिष्ठानप्रधानपूर्वकत्वं व्यापकम् । तच्चात्र नास्ति । सत्यजगद्द्वयाङ्गीकारादस्यैव जगतः सत्यत्वाङ्गीकारस्य लघुत्वात् । अतो व्याप्यकल्पनापि नास्तीति प्रमाणविरोधः ।

२७०. तथा च प्रयोगः—प्रपञ्चो न भ्रान्तिकल्पितः, निरधिष्ठानत्वान्निष्प्रधानत्वादात्मवद्व्यतिरेकेण वा रजतवत् । विपक्षे त्वारोप्यसदृशाधिष्ठानप्रधानभूतसत्यजगद्द्वयाङ्गीरप्रसङ्गो बाधकः ।

268. Therefore, the universe is not posited as delusive, (and) hence the inference through cognisability, etc., (as probans) is refuted by counter-arguments (*reductio ad absurdum*).

269. Further, for assumptiveness, there is a pervader, *viz.*, being preceded by a substrate and archetype that are similar to the super-imposed. And they (the substrate and the archetype) do not exist here (in the subject). For, it is more consistent with parsimony to admit the reality of this universe than to admit two real universes. Therefore even the pervaded *viz.* assumptiveness does not exist; hence, there is conflict with the means of valid knowledge.

270. And there is the syllogism thus: "The universe is not delusively posited, because it has neither a substrate nor an archetype, like the self; or negatively like the silver (cognised in the shell-silver delusion)." On the contrary view, there is the sublater in the form of the contingence of the admission of two real

२७१. ननु यदुक्तम्—यद्भ्रान्तिकल्पितं तत्साधिष्ठानमिति तन्न; स्वाप्नपदार्थे व्यभिचारात्। तथाहि—स्वाप्नास्तावत् पदार्था भ्रान्तिकल्पिताः। सत्यत्वे हि तेऽनादिनित्या उतोत्पत्तिविनाशवन्तः।

२७२. आद्ये प्रागूर्ध्वं चोपलभ्येरन्। द्वितीये किं न बोधानन्तरमुपलभ्यन्ते।

२७३. तदैवोत्पद्य विनष्टा इति चेन्न; असंभावितत्वात्। किञ्चैवमुपादानानि निमित्तानि चोपलब्धव्यानि।

universes, that are substrate and archetype and are similar to what is super-imposed.

XXXI

271. Now, what has been said, "that which is delusively posited has a substrate," that is not (true), because there is the inconstancy (of the probans) in respect of the dream-object. It is as follows: now, (all) the objects (cognised) in dream are delusively posited. Indeed, if they be real, they are either beginningless and eternal or they are created and destroyed.

272. In the first case, they should be cognised both earlier and later. In the second case, why is it that they are not cognised after waking?

273. If it be said that they are born and destroyed then alone (in the dream), no (says the Advaitin), because of impossibility. Further, in this way the material and the efficient causes (of the dream-objects) have to be known.

२७४. अपि चैतानन्तः पश्यति बहिर्वा ? नाद्यः, अल्पप्रदेशे महतां दर्शनासंभवात् । नोत्तरः ; पार्श्वस्थानामप्युपलम्भप्रसङ्गात् ।

२७५. केन चैते करणेनोपलभ्यन्ते । न तावद्बाह्येन्द्रियैः, तेषां तदोपरतत्वात् । नापि मनसा ; तस्य बहिरस्वातन्त्र्यात् ।

२७६. किञ्च काश्यां सुप्तो मधुरां पश्यति ; तथा हेमन्ते सुप्तो वसन्तम् । न च तत्र तयोः सम्भवः । तस्माद्भ्रान्तिकल्पिताः ।

२७७. न चात्र किञ्चिदधिष्ठानमस्ति, आत्मनो भेदेनोपलम्भात् । न ह्यहं गज इति तदा प्रतीतिरस्तीति ।

274. Further, these objects (in dreams), are they cognised inside (the body) or outside? Not the first, because it is impossible to cognise huge objects in a small place. Not the latter, because of the contingence of cognition even by the people by one's side.

275. And by what instrument are these (dream-objects) cognised? Now, it is not by the outer sense-organs, because at that time they are (all) at rest. Nor is it by the mind (manas) because it has no independent power (of cognition) outside (the body).

276. Further, one asleep in Benares (Kāśī) perceives Madura (in his dream). Likewise one who sleeps in autumn (experiences) spring. And of these, there is no possibility at that (time or) place. Therefore they are delusively posited.

277. Nor is there any substrate here; for the self is cognised as different (from the objects of the dream). Indeed the cognition is, then, not in the from "I am an elephant".

२७८. एतदप्यविमर्शसुन्दरम्, तेषां सत्यत्वात्। तेन निरधिष्ठानत्वेऽपि न विरोधः।

२७९. ननु सत्यत्वे बाधकमुक्तम्। मैवम्; उत्पत्तिविनाशाङ्गीकारात्।

२८०. न च प्रागूर्ध्वमुपलम्भप्रसङ्गः, विद्युदादिवत्तात्कालिकत्वसम्भवात्।

२८१. तर्ह्युपादानाद्युपलब्धिः स्यादिति चेन्न; वासनोपादानकत्वात्। वासनानां चातीन्द्रियत्वादनुपलब्धिर्युज्यते। निमित्तादिकं त्वदृष्टेश्वरादिकमिति।

278. This too has charm (only) for the unreflective, because those (objects seen in dreams) are real, (says the siddhāntin). Hence, there is nothing contradictory (to our argument) even if they do not have a substrate.

279. Now, the sublater has been set forth in (regarding them as) real. It is not so (says the siddhāntin), because of the acceptance of production and destruction (for the dream-objects).

280. Nor is there the contingence of the cognition of (dream-objects) before (and) after; for instantaneousness is possible, as for lightning, etc.

281. If it be said that there should in that case be the cognition of the material cause, etc., no (says siddhāntin); for, impressions are the material cause. And impressions being supersensible, their not being cognised stands to reason. The efficient cause, etc. are the unseen (potency), God, etc.

२८२. अतीन्द्रियकार्यस्यापि त्र्यणुकवदुपलम्भः सम्भवति। अत एवान्तर्मनस उपलब्धिर्युज्यते।

२८३. निरधिष्ठानत्वमसिद्धम्, आत्मनोऽधिष्ठानत्वादिति चेन्न; आत्मनोऽधिष्ठानत्वासंभवात्।

२८४. नात्मा जगदारोपाधिष्ठानम्; अविषयत्वात्; तद्विरुद्धतया प्रतीयमानत्वात्; यथा पर्वतो न सर्षपारोपाधिष्ठानम्।

२८५. प्रपञ्चो वा नात्मन्यध्यस्तः, तद्विरुद्धतया प्रतीयमानत्वात्; यथा सर्षपो न पर्वतेऽध्यस्तः।

282. Cognition is possible of the product of even what is supersensible, as (in the case of) the Triad. Hence too, cognition by the mind within (the body) stands to reason.

283. If it be said that (the probans) "the non-existence of substrate" is not established, since the self is the substrate, no (says the siddhāntin), because the self cannot possibly be the substrate.

284. The self is not the substrate of the super-imposition of the world, because it is not a content (of cognition), since it is cognised as the opposite of that (*i.e.*, content), like the mountain not being the substrate of the super-imposition of the mustard seed.

285. Nor is the universe superimposed on the self, because it is cognised as the opposite of that (*i.e.*, self) just as the mustard seed is not superimposed on the mountain.

२८६. विरुद्धाकारप्रतीतावध्यासाङ्गीकारे तस्य कदाप्यनिवृत्तिप्रसङ्गः ।

२८७. किञ्च यदि जगदात्मन्यारोपितं स्यात्तदात्मनो भिन्नत्वेन न दृश्येत । यद्यत्रारोपितं तत्ततो भिन्नत्वेन न प्रतीयते । यथा शुक्तिकायामारोपितं रजतं न शुक्तिकाया भिन्नत्वेन प्रतीयते भ्रान्तौ । दृश्यते चेदमिदानीं जगदात्मनो भिन्नत्वेन । तस्मान्न तत्रारोपितमिति ।

२८८. किञ्च ब्रह्मणि प्रपञ्चस्यारोपितत्वं वदन्नन्यत्र प्रपञ्चस्य सत्तामङ्गीकरोति न वा ?

२८९. आद्ये, परस्य मिथ्यात्वप्रतिज्ञाहानिः । न चेत्कस्य कुत्रारोपः । न हि शशविषाणं क्वचिदारोप्यते ।

286. If the super-imposition be admitted (even) where there is cognition of an opposite form, there is the contingence of its (illusion) being non-removable at any time (says the siddhāntin).

287. Further, if the universe be superimposed on the self, then it would not be cognised as different from the self. Where one is super-imposed on another, that (former) is not cognised as different from that (latter), just as the silver superimposed on the shell is not cognised as different from the shell, in delusion. And this universe is now cognised as different from the self. Hence it is not superimposed thereon.

288. Besides, in saying that the universe is superimposed on Brahman, do they admit the reality of the universe elsewhere, or do they not?

289. In the first case, there is the abandonment of the premised illusoriness of the latter (universe).

२९०. नास्माभिरन्यत्र सतः प्रपञ्चस्य ब्रह्मण्यारोपोऽभिधीयते येन सर्वमिथ्यात्वप्रतिज्ञाहानिरापद्येत । किन्त्वनिर्वचनीयरूपः कश्चिदनात्माकारोऽयं प्रपञ्चो ब्रह्मण्यारोपित इत्यङ्गीक्रियते इति चेन्न ।

२९१. अनात्माकारः प्रपञ्च इति कोऽर्थः? किमात्मनोऽन्य? उतात्मविरुद्धः? उतात्माभावो वा?

२९२. नाद्यद्वितीयौ; कचित्प्रपञ्चस्य सत्यतापातात् । न तृतीयः; आत्मन्यात्माभावारोपस्य काप्यदृष्टत्वात् । न हि कश्चिदहमहं न भवामीति भ्रान्तो दृश्यते ।

If there is no (such reality of the universe elsewhere), of what is the super-imposition and where? There is indeed no super-imposition somewhere of the horns of the hare.

290. "By us (Advaitins) is not declared the super-imposition of a universe, which is real elsewhere, on Brahman, in which case, there would result the abandonment of the premised illusoriness of every thing. It is on the other hand admitted that the universe, which is something indeterminable by nature and of the form of the not-self is superimposed on Brahman." If this be said, no (says the siddhāntin).

291. What is the meaning of (the expression) "the universe of the form of the not-self"? Is it other than the self, or opposed to the self, or the non-existence of the self?

292. It is not the first and the second because of the contingence of the reality of the universe in some place. Not the third, because the super-imposition

२९३. विमत आत्मा आत्माभावारोपाधिष्ठानं न भवति ; आत्मत्वाद्देवदत्तवत् ।

२९४. ननु निष्प्रधानत्वमसिद्धम् ; पूर्वपूर्वप्रपञ्चस्योत्तरोत्तरप्रपञ्चारोपे प्रधानत्वादिति चेन्न ; असत्वात् । एवमनेकानुमानप्रतिहतत्वान्न दृश्यत्वानुमानं समञ्जसमिति सिद्धम् ।

२९५. अस्य पटस्यावयवित्वादिनैतत्तन्तुनिष्ठात्यन्ताभावप्रतियोगित्वसाधनमप्यत्यन्ताभावस्य निष्प्रतियोगिकत्वेन बाधितम् ।

of the non-existence of the self in the self is nowhere cognised. Indeed, no one is found to have the delusion " I am not myself ".

293. The self under dispute cannot become the substrate of the super-imposition of the non-existence of the self, because it is the self, like Devadatta.

294. Now, if it be said that (the probans) " not having an archetype " is not established, because each prior universe is the archetype for every subsequent super-imposition of the universe, no (says the siddhāntin), because of unreality. Since in this way the inference with (the probans) " cognisability " is refuted by many an inference it is established that it (the inference) is not sound.

XXXII

295. Even the establishment of this cloth being the counter-correlate of the absolute non-existence present in these threads through its being what has

२९६. एतत्तन्तुषु नास्तीति साधने सिद्धसाधनम् ; कार्यकारणयोरभेदेनाधाराधेयभावाभावात् ।

२९७. एतत्तन्तुकार्यं न भवतीति साधनेऽकार्यत्वस्यान्यकार्यत्वस्य वा सिद्ध्यार्थान्तरत्वम् । आकाशादिषु चैवंप्रयोगाभावेन सर्वजगन्मिथ्यात्वासिद्धिश्च ।

२९८. किञ्च किमत्र पटस्यासत्त्वमापाद्यते ? संसर्गनिषेधो वा क्रियते ? नाद्यः ; त्वद्दर्शनविरोधात् ।

the parts (*i.e.*, the whole) etc., is sublated by absolute non-existence not having a counter-correlate.

296. In establishing that it (the cloth) does not exist in these threads, there is (the defect of) the establishment of the established; for, there being non-difference of cause and effect, there is the non-existence of the relation of the container and the contained.

297. In inferring "this is not the effect of threads" there is something else (proved) by establishing non-produccdness, or production by something else. And because of the inapplicability of such syllogism to ether, etc., there is the non-establishment of illusoriness in respect of the entire universe.

XXXIII

298. Besides, here is there adduced the unreality of the cloth or is there denied the relation (of the cloth to the threads)? Not the first, because it is opposed to your (Advaitin's) school of thought.

२९९. सत्त्वमात्रं निषिध्यते, नासत्त्वमापाद्यते इति चेन्न ; तन्निषेधे तद्ध्रौव्यात् । सत्त्वनिषेधे चैतत्तन्तुनिष्ठपदवैयर्थ्यम् ।

३००. न च सिद्धसाधनतापरिहारार्थं विशेषणमिति वक्तव्यम् । एतत्पटात्यन्ताभावस्यास्माकमसिद्धेः । एतेन दृष्टान्तोऽपि साध्यविकलतया प्रत्युक्तो वेदितव्यः ।

३०१. ननु पटान्तरस्यात्यन्ताभावो न चेत्, पटः किं न स्यात् ? किमत्र पटसंसर्गः स्यात्पटो वा ?

३०२. आद्ये व्याप्त्यसिद्धिः । द्वितीये सिद्धसाधनम् ।

299. If it be said that reality alone is denied, but that unreality is not adduced, it is not so (says the siddhāntin); for, when that (reality) is denied there is stability for that (unreality). And if reality be denied, there would be the futility of the words "present in these threads."

300. Nor may it be said that the attribute is (used) to remove (the defect of) the establishment of the established; for the absolute non-existence of this cloth is not established for us (the Dvaitins). By this, the example too is to be understood to have been refuted as devoid of the probandum.

301. Now, (asks the objector) if of another cloth there is no absolute non-existence (in these threads), then why should not that other cloth exist (there)? Here, (asks the siddhāntin), would there be the relationship with the cloth, or the cloth (itself)?

302. In the first case, there is no establishment of the pervasion. In the second case, there is (the defect of) the establishment of the established.

३०३. नाप्युत्तरः ; तन्तुपटसंसर्गाभावस्य सिद्धत्वात् ।

३०४. अथायं पट एतत्तन्तुजन्यो न भवतीति प्रतिज्ञावाक्यार्थः स्यात् तर्हि तस्यांशित्वमपि न स्यादिति हेतोरसिद्धिः स्यात् ।

३०५. न तत्त्वतस्तदप्यस्तीति चेन्न ; अतात्त्विकावयवित्वस्यास्माकमसिद्धेः । इह तन्तुषु पट इत्यादिप्रत्यक्षविरुद्धं चैतत् ।

३०६. नन्विह नभसि नीलिमेति प्रत्यक्षाभिमतप्रत्ययबाधेनारूपित्वानुमानप्रवृत्तिवदत्रानुमानप्रवृत्त्युपपत्तिः किं न स्यादिति चेन्न ।

303. Not the latter too (*i.e.*, denial of relation). For the non-existence of the relation between the threads and the cloth is established.

304. If, then, the meaning of the premised statement is "this cloth is not produced out of those threads", in that case, it would not even be (the probans) "what has the parts"; so there would be the non-establishment of the probans.

305. If it be said that in reality that too is not there, no (says the siddhāntin); for "being what has the parts and non-real" is not established for us (Dvaitins). And this is in conflict with such perceptions as "here in the threads there is cloth".

306. Now if it be asked, "like the functioning of the inference of colourlessness sublating what is considered the perceptual cognition of blueness here in the sky, here too why should not the functioning of inference be intelligible?" no (says siddhāntin).

३०७. तथा सति दहनशैत्यानुमानादेरप्यप्रतिबद्धप्रसरेण बाधपरिभाषापरिमोषापातात् ।

३०८. उभयवादिसम्प्रतिपन्नप्रामाण्ये प्रत्यक्षादौ जाग्रति बाधः सुखं प्रसरेदिति चेत्—तर्त्कि प्रकृते प्रत्यक्षप्रामाण्यानभ्युपगमे कारणम् ?

३०९. अनुमानविरोध इति चेत्समं दहनशैत्यानुमानेऽपि । न च प्रत्यक्षस्यानुमानबाधितत्वे दृष्टान्तं पश्यामः । नभोनीलिमप्रतीतिभ्रमताप्यागमाद्यवगम्यैव, अनुमानस्याप्रसरात् ।

३१०. तथाहि महत्वान्नभसो रूपं निषिध्यते, अगन्धवत्वाद्वा, स्पर्शरहितत्वाद्वा । न त्रयमपि ; तत एवाशब्दत्वप्रसङ्गात् ।

307. If so, when even inferences like (the one) that establishes coldness of fire function unhindered, there will result the doing away with the nomenclature of sublation.

308. If it be said that sublation can function easily while there remains awake perception, etc., whose validity is accepted by both the disputants, then, in the present case, what is the cause for not accepting the validity of perception ?

309. If it be said that it is the conflict with inference, it is the same even in the inference of the coldness of fire. And we know of no example, where perception is sublated by inference. Even the delusiveness of the cognition of the blue colour in the sky is known only through scripture, since inference does not function here.

310. It is thus : is the blue colour of the sky denied because it is gross (mahatvāt), or because it

३११. अथ तत्रागमविरोधः, तर्ह्यरूपित्वमपि तस्यागमसिद्धमेव, नानुमानादिति । तस्मात्कालातीततादोषं कचित्स्वीकुर्वतात्रापि समानन्याय-तया सा चाभ्युपेयैव ।

३१२. किञ्च जगतो मिथ्यात्वाभावे न बाधकं पश्यामः । सत्यत्वे कथं प्रकाशेत । न तावत्स्वतः, जडत्वात् । नापि परतः, प्रकाशान्तरेण सम्बन्धाभावात् । असम्बद्धस्य प्रकाशनेऽतिप्रसङ्गात् ।

is devoid of smell, or because it is devoid of touch? Not any one of the three, since even from this (probans) there is the contingence of denying (the quality of) sound (in respect of the ether).

311. If (then) there is contradiction (for the inference that establishes the fact that sky is not the abode of sound) by scripture, then its colourlessness too certainly results from scripture, not from inference. And therefore by (him) who accepts the defect of adducing (the probans) after the lapse of the (proper) time (*i.e.* sublation), in some place, that (defect) must necessarily be accepted here too (in the present case) by parity of reasoning.

XXXIV

312. Besides, we (the Dvaitins) do not know of any sublater in (accepting) the non-existence of the illusoriness of the universe. If real, how can it be manifest? Not by its own self, because it is inert; nor by another, because there is non-existence of relation with another manifestor. If what is non-related (to a

३१३. असत्त्वे तु चित्प्रकाशारोपितस्याधिष्ठानाध्यस्तत्वसम्बन्धेन प्रकाशोपपत्तिरिति चेन्न; विचारागोचरत्वात् ।

३१४. तथाहि—कथं प्रकाशेतेति कोऽर्थः? कथं प्रकाशः स्यादिति वा? कथं प्रकाशाश्रय इति वा? कथं प्रकाशविषय इति वा?

३१५. न प्रथमद्वितीयौ; अनभ्युपगमात् । तृतीयेऽपि किं प्रकाशशब्देन चैतन्यं विवक्षितम्? वृत्तिर्वा?

३१६. नाद्य; चैतन्याविषयत्वेऽपि बाधकाभावात्; वृत्तिविषय-

manifestor) should manifest, then there would be (the defect of) undue extension.

313. "If, however, it is (regarded as) unreal (illusory) its manifestation is intelligible by the relation of substrate and super-imposition thereon for (the universe) which is superimposed on the self-luminous consciousness;" if this be said, no (says the siddhāntin); for it is beyond the sphere of (comprehension by) inquiry.

314. It is as follows: what is the meaning of "how can it be manifest"? Is it (1) "how does it become manifest"? (2) "or how is it the substrate of manifestation?" or (3) "how is it the content of manifestation?"

315. Not the first and the second, because they are not accepted. In the third too, is "consciousness," or "psychosis" the meaning intended by the word "manifestation"?

316. Not the first; for, though not the content of consciousness, there is no sublater, since, even with

त्वेनैव व्यवहारोपपत्तेः । चैतन्यस्यापि स्वाभाविकं भविष्यतीति को दोषः ?

३१७. असङ्गश्रुतिस्तु परमेश्वरस्य पापादिसम्बन्धाभाववादिनी ।

३१८. न द्वितीयः, करणसामर्थ्येन विषयविषयिभावोपपत्तेः ।

३१९. किञ्च अध्यस्तत्वेन प्रकाशने जीवेऽध्यासपक्षे सर्वदा प्रकाशः स्यात् । ब्रह्मण्यध्यासे न कदाचित् ।

३२०. बहुजीवपक्षेऽपि जीवेऽध्यासे सर्वदा सर्वेषां प्रपञ्चः प्रकाशेत । ब्रह्माधिष्ठानत्वे तु न कस्यापि कदापि ।

being the content of the psychosis, the empirical usage (of immediacy) is intelligible. (Again) what is the defect in (regarding) consciousness too as (manifesting what is) naturally (related to it, not only what is super-imposed thereon)?

317. On the other hand, as for the scriptural statement of non-relation (of the Purusa), that is to be taken as declaring the non-existence of relatedness of sin, etc. to the supreme Lord.

318. Not the second, because by the efficiency of the instrument there is intelligibility (secured) for the subject-object relation (between the psychosis and the world).

319. Besides, if the manifestation by super-imposition be on the view that the super-imposition is in the individual self (Jiva), there would be manifestation at all times. On the view of super-imposition on Brahman, never (would there be manifestation).

320. Even on the view of a plurality of individual selves, if the super-imposition be on the individual self,

३२१. तथापि सत्यत्वे दृश्यत्वं न युज्यते दृग्दृश्ययोः संसर्गनिरूपणादिति चेन्न ।

३२२. संयोगासम्भवे समवायवदन्यस्यापि तयोरसम्भवे कल्प्यत्वात्, विषयविषयिभावस्य सम्भवात् ।

३२३. न च तदनिरूपणम् । ज्ञानजन्यफलाधारत्वलक्षणं तत्तत्प्रतीतियोग्यत्वं विषयत्वमस्त्विति चेत—तत्फलं ज्ञातता व्यवहारो वा ?

३२४. नाद्यः ; अतीतादौ तदसंभवेनाविषयत्वापत्तेः । न द्वितीयः, गगनादावभावादिति ।

the world would be manifest to all at all times; if the substrate, however, be Brahman, to no one and at no time (would it be manifest).

321. If it be said that even then, if (the universe is) real, cognisability (as probans) would not be appropriate, since no relation is demonstrated as between cognition and the cognised, no (says the siddhāntin).

322. For, just as inherence (is assumed) where conjunction is impossible, there may be assumed even another relation, when these two are not possible (and) hence the subject-object relation is possible.

323. "Nor is it undemonstrated. To be respectively fit for different cognitions, as being the substrate of the fruit generated by (those) cognitions, let this be (the definition of) being the content of cognition;" if this be said, is the fruit cognisedness or empirical usage?

324. Not the first; for this being impossible in past objects, etc., there is the contingence of their being

३२५. मैवम्; अतीतादौ ज्ञातताभ्युपगमे विरोधाभावात्; अन्यथा तद्व्यवहारायोगात्।

३२६. अतीतादावनुगतविषयत्वं नास्तीति चेत्, प्रतिनियतमेवास्तु।

३२७. व्यवहारोऽपि तत्तद्योग्यमेव ज्ञानजन्यफलं किं न स्यात्? तस्मान्नानुमानं विश्वमिथ्यात्वे मानम्।

३२८. ननु सत्यत्वे प्रपञ्चो ब्रह्मणो भिन्नः? अभिन्नः? भिन्नाभिन्नः? भिन्नाभिन्नविलक्षणो वा?

not the content of cognition. Not the second, because it is not found in respect of sky, etc. (which cannot be taken up, rejected, etc.).

325. Not so (says the siddhāntin); for, in the acceptance of cognisedness in respect of past objects, etc., there is no conflict; because, otherwise there is impossibility of empirical usage in respect of them.

326. If it be said that in respect of past objects, etc., there is no common contentness (viṣayatvam), (then) let it be different for each (class of objects), (says the siddhāntin).

327. Why should there not be empirical usage also as cognition-generated fruit suited to respective capacities? Therefore inference is not an authority in respect of the illusoriness of the universe.,

XXXV.

328. "Now, if the universe is real, is it different from Brahman, or non-different (from Brahman), or

३२९. आद्ये भेदपरम्परयानवस्था । द्वितीयेऽपसिद्धान्तः । तृतीये व्याघातः । चतुर्थेऽनिर्वाच्यता—इति चेन्न; भेदस्य स्वरूपत्वेनानवस्थाया अभावात् ।

३३०. किञ्चैवं सति ब्रह्मण्यपि प्रपञ्चाद्भिन्नमभिन्नं वेत्यादिदोषाः समा एव ।

३३१. "नेह नाना" इत्यागमोऽस्तु विश्वमिथ्यात्वे मानमिति चेन्न; तस्य ब्रह्मणि नानात्वनिषेधपरत्वात् ।

different and non-different, or other than different and non-different?

329. "In the first case, through the chain of differences, there is infinite regress. In the second case, there is opposition to one's own doctrine. In the third case, there is contradiction. In the fourth case, there is indeterminability." If this be said, no (says the siddhāntin). For, difference being the very nature (of the thing) there is non-existence of infinite regress.

330. Further, in this case, there is certainly parity of such defects, even (in questions) as to whether Brahman is different or non-different from the world.

XXXVI

331. If it be said "Let scriptural statements like 'Here there is no manifoldness (Neha nānā)', etc., be the authority in respect of the illusoriness of the universe," no, (says the siddhāntin); for, that (scriptural statement) has for purport the denial of manifoldness in Brahman.

३३२. न ब्रह्मणि नानात्वं प्रसक्तं यन्निषेध्यते इति चेत्; हन्त! तथा सति त्वयाप्येकमेवाद्वितीयमित्यादेः स्वगतनानात्वनिषेधपरत्वमभ्युपगतं कथं स्यात्; अखण्डवादानारम्भप्रसङ्गाच्च ।

३३३. नानाशब्दस्य भावप्रत्ययान्तताभावान्नेति चेन्न; "मुक्तोपसृप्यव्यपदेशात्" इत्यादौ भावप्रत्ययाभावेऽपि तदर्थदर्शनात् ।

३३४. तर्हि "एकमेवाद्वितीयम्" इत्यागमोऽस्तु मानमत्रेति चेन्न; अद्वितीयपदस्य सजातीयवस्त्वन्तरनिषेधपरत्वात् ।

332. "In Brahman there is no contingence of manifoldness, which could be denied." If this be said, alas! (says the siddhāntin) in that case, how can it be accepted by you (Advaitin) that the denial of the manifoldness present in (Brahman) itself is the purport of such (texts) as "(Brahman is) one only without a second?" And (it is so) because there is the contingence of non-commencement of the discussion of the impartite (sense), (since according to the Advaitin there is no contingence of difference in Brahman).

333. If it be said that as in the word manifoldness (nānā) there is the non-existence of the termination (implying the sense) of an abstract noun, it is not so, no (says the siddhāntin); for, even in the absence of a suffix conveying the sense of an abstract noun, in the aphorism. "Because of the teaching of being the object that is attained by the released selves (Muktopasṛpyavyapades'āt)" there is seen that sense (of an abstract noun).

334. Then, if it be said that revealed statements (āgama) like "one only without a second", can be

३३५. एकत्वविशेषणेनैव सजातीयस्य निषिद्धत्वान्नैवमिति चेन्न; तस्यैकत्वसंख्याविधानपरत्वात् ।

३३६. एका संख्यैकोऽभाव इत्यादिप्रयोगासम्भवो नास्मान् प्रति प्रौढिमावहति ।

३३७. अनन्तपदं च देशकालान्तवत्त्वाभावपरम्; तत्रैव व्युत्पन्नत्वात् ।

३३८. अन्तशब्दस्य देशतः कालतो वस्तुतः परिच्छिन्ने व्युत्पन्न-

the authority here (in respect of the illusoriness of the universe), no (says the siddhāntin), because, the expression "without a second" has for purport the denial of another entity of the same class.

335. If it be said that it is not so, since the denial (of another) of the same class is secured even by the attribute, one (only), no (says the siddhāntin); for it (the word, one) has got for purport the affirmation of unity in number.

336. The impossibility of usages like "the number is one", "non-existence is one", does not convey any challenge to us (since unlike Logicians—Tarkikas —we do not hold that qualities, inherence, etc., can have no qualities and that substance alone can have qualities like number).

337. And the word unlimited (ananta) has for purport (only) the non-existence of limitation in space and time; for that alone is its etymological significance.

338. "Since the word, limit (anta) has for its etymological significance, 'what is limited in space or

त्वात्तस्य नञ्समासे त्रिविधस्याप्यन्तस्य निषेधकत्वोपपत्तौ पृथग्व्युत्पत्तिर्नापेक्षितेति चेन्न; अन्तशब्दस्योक्तत्रयेऽव्युत्पन्नत्वादिति। तस्मात्सत्यभेदचेतनाचेतनात्मनो विश्वस्य हरिः कर्तेति निराबाधमवस्थितम्।

३३९. ननु कथं भेदसत्यता युक्तिमती? "विमता आत्मानः परमात्मनः परमार्थतो न भिद्यन्ते; आत्मत्वात्, परमात्मवत्" इत्यनुमानेन विरोधादिति चेन्न; आत्मत्वस्य प्रागेव निरस्तत्वात्।

in time, or by (another) object, when there is a compound (formed) with the negative particle, (therewith) it is intelligible that there is denial of even all the three limitations; hence there is no necessity for a separate etymology (for the word unlimited)". If this be said, no (says the siddhāntin); for, the word unlimited has no etymological significance is respect of all the said three (senses), (but only in respect of the first two). Therefore, it is established without any obstruction that of the world of real differences, of the form of the sentients and the non-sentients, Hari is the creator.

XXXVII

339. Now, how does the reality of difference stand to reason, since (that difference) is in conflict with the inference "the selves (Ātmans) under dispute are not in reality different from the supreme self (Paramātman) because of self-hood (Ātmatva) like the supreme self (Paramātman)"? If this be asked, no (says the siddhāntin), because (the probans) self-hood has been already refuted.

३४०. अस्तु तर्हि—

विमतं तात्त्विकस्वान्तर्भेदहीनं मतत्वतः ।
यदित्थं तत्तथा यद्वत्खं तथेदं ततस्तथा ॥

इत्यनुमानविरोध इति चेन्न, विचारागोचरत्वात् ।

३४१. तथाहि—किमत्र स्वान्तर्भेदहीनताशब्देन प्रत्येकं पदार्थानां स्वगतभेदराहित्यमुच्यते ? उत भेदाधिकरणत्वविरहः ?

३४२. नाद्यः ; सिद्धसाधनत्वात् । नोत्तरः ; साध्यविकलत्वाद्दृष्टान्तस्य ।

340. "The thing under dispute is devoid of real difference within itself, because it is cognisable; that which is thus (cognisable) is so (devoid of real difference), like ether; so is this (thing in dispute); therefore it is so.

Let the conflict be with this inference." If this be said, no (says the siddhāntin); for, it cannot stand inquiry.

341. It is thus: here by the expression "devoid of difference within itself", is there stated separately the non-existence of difference of each thing from itself, or (the thing) being devoid of (the quality) substrateness of difference?

342. Not the first, because of (the defect of) the establishment of the established. Not the latter, since the example is devoid of the probandum.

३४३. यथाकाशस्य स्वगतो भेदो नास्ति तथा जगदाख्ये पदार्थ-समुदायेऽपि न तादृशभेद इति चेत्—अत्रापि कोऽर्थः ? यथाकाशस्याप्याकाशप्रतियोगिको भेदो नास्ति तथा जगतोऽपि तत्प्रतियोगिको भेदो नेत्यर्थाभ्युपगमे सिद्धसाधनम् ।

३४४. अथ यथा घटाकाशमठाकाशयोर्न भेदः, तथा जगदंशयोरपीति चेन्न; साध्यविकलत्वाद्दृष्टान्तस्य । व्योम्नोऽपि संयोगित्वेन सावयवत्वसाधनादित्यलम् ।

343. If it be said that just as the ether has no difference in itself, likewise the totality of things which goes under the name "universe" also has no such difference, here too, what is the meaning? "Just as the ether has no difference having the ether as its counter-correlate, likewise the universe also has no difference, having that (world itself) as its counter-correlate". If this be the meaning accepted, there is (the defect of) the establishment of the established.

344. If then, it be said that just as there is no difference between the ether delimited by a pot and ether delimited by a monastry (Muṭha) likewise there is no difference even between the parts of the universe, no (says the siddhāntin), since, the example is devoid of the probandum; for, even of the ether (as for pot, etc.) possession of parts is established, because of having conjunction (with others). Hence, enough (of this).

३४५. भेदो मिथ्या भेदत्वाच्चन्द्रभेदवदित्यनुमानमस्त्विति चेन्न; साध्यानिरुक्तेः। दृष्टान्ते साधनविकलत्वञ्च। तत्र तद्भेदासत्त्वेन भेदत्वस्यैवाभावात्।

३४६. परमार्थतस्तदभावेऽपि कथञ्चिदस्ति भेदः; अतो भेदत्वमपीति चेन्न; तादृशस्य भेदत्वस्य पक्षेऽनन्वयात्।

३४७. अवधूयैव बाधितत्वादिविशेषं भेदत्वसामान्यस्यैव हेतुतेति चेन्न।

XXXVIII

345. If it be said that there can be the inference, "difference is illusory, because of the nature of difference, like the difference of the moon (when delusively perceived as double)" no (says the siddhāntin), since the probandum is not defined; and the example too is devoid of probans; for difference from there itself being unreal, the very nature of difference is non-existent.

346. If it be said that though there is the non-existence of that (difference) as absolutely real, difference does exist somehow and consequently also the nature of difference, no (says the siddhāntin); for, a difference of such a character is not related to the subject.

347. If it be said that leaving out special features like sublatedness, etc., the generic character of difference is alone the probans, no (says the siddhāntin).

३४८. धूमबाष्पयोर्धूमत्ववत्सामान्यस्याप्यभावात् । अन्यथानवधारितबाधितत्वाबाधितत्वादिविशेषेण धूमवत्वमात्रेण ह्रदादेरपि सदहनतापातात् ।

३४९. अप्रमाणगम्यत्वमुपाधिश्च । भेदत्वादेव तदपि स्यादिति चेन्न ; प्रातिभासिकत्वस्याप्यापातात् ।

३५०. अथात्र व्यवहारनिर्वाहकता प्रतीयते इति चेत्—तर्ह्यत्र प्रत्यक्षादिप्रमाणसिद्धतां च किन्न पश्यसि ?

348. For in the case of smoke and vapour, a generic nature too is as much non-existent as smokeness (common to both). Otherwise, through the mere smokeness not ascertained to be particularised as sublated or unsublated or otherwise there is the contingence of (the inference of) even a lake, etc., containing fire.

XXXIX

349. And "being not cognised by a means of valid knowledge" is the adjunct. If it be said that that too is only because of being of the nature of difference, no (says the siddhāntin); for there is the contingence even of the nature of mere appearance.

350. If then it be said that there is the cognition of being what brings about empirical usage in respect of that (difference), then, why do you not see also its being established by means of a valid knowledge like perception, etc. ?

३५१. ननु कथं प्रत्यक्षस्य भेदग्राहकत्वम्? तत्किं भेदमेव गोचरयेदुत वस्त्वपि?

३५२. नाद्यः; धर्मिप्रतियोगिप्रतीतिमन्तरेण भेदप्रतिपत्तेरयोगात्।

३५३. द्वितीये किं भेदपूर्वं वस्तु वस्तुपूर्वं वा भेदं युगपद्वोभयं गोचरयेत्?

३५४. नाद्यः; दत्तोत्तरत्वात्। न द्वितीयः; बुद्धेर्विरम्यव्यापारायोगात्। नापि तृतीयः; कार्यकारणबुद्ध्योर्यौगपद्यायोगात्।

३५५. तत्तद्भेदस्य भेदान्तरभेदेऽनवस्थानम्। अनन्तभेदाभ्युपगमेऽपि मूलक्षतेरभावान्नानवस्थादोष इति चेन्न।

XL

351. Now, how can perception lead to the cognition of difference? Does that (perception) have as sphere the difference alone or the thing (*i.e.*, the substrate of the difference) too?

352. Not the first, because it is impossible to have the cognition of difference, without the cognition of the substrate and the counter-correlate.

353. In the second case, does it have as sphere (*i.e.* cognise) the difference prior to the thing, or the thing prior to difference or both simultaneously?

354. Not the first, because the reply has been already given. Not the second, because delayed functioning is impossible for the intellect. Not the third also, because simultaneity is impossible for two cognitions that are cause and effect.

355. If a particular difference (say between the cloth and pot) from the differents (be recognised)

३५६. अयमितो भिन्न इति वानयोर्भेद इति वा?

३५७. नाद्यः; विशिष्टत्वेनैव प्रतीतिनियमात्। न द्वितीयः, भेदेनैव विज्ञातस्य विशेषणत्वात्।

३५८. ततश्च पूर्वपूर्वभेदप्रतीतिमन्तरेणोत्तरोत्तरभेदाप्रतीतेरनन्तत्वायुगपत्प्रतीतेरयोगाच्च मूलक्षतेरनवस्था सुस्थैवेति।

through another difference, there is infinite regress. If it be said that since even on the acceptance of infinite differences there is non-existence of (the defect)) of cutting-at-the-root (of the argument), the infinite regress is not a defect, no (says the Advaitin).

356. (In what form is difference cognised,) whether as "this is different from that", or as "there is difference between these two"?

357. Not the first, because of the invariability of the cognition (as "this" and "that") being only as qualified (by difference), (so that cognition of difference, and the cognition of its substrate pre-suppose each other in an endless series). Not the second, because the qualification ("between these two") is only what is (already) cognised as different.

358. Therefore, since each later difference is not cognised in the absence of the congnition of the prior difference, because of the infinitude (of these) and because the simultaneous cognition (of these) is impossible, there is the cutting-at-the-root (of the argument); hence infinite regress is certainly well established (as a defect).

३५९. विद्यमानभेदस्य स्वरूपेण गृहीतस्य विशेषणतोपपत्तौ किं भेदाप्रतीतिः करिष्यतीति चेन्न ।

३६०. दूरस्थवनस्पत्योः क्षीरनीरयोर्वा स्वरूपतो विद्यमानभेदयोरपि स्फुरतोः संयुक्तत्वादिप्रतीत्यदर्शनात् ।

३६१. तत्र समानाभिघातदोषादप्रतीतिरिति चेन्न; विद्यमानभेदयोः स्वरूपेण स्फुरतोर्विशेषणविशेष्यभावग्रहणस्थलस्य सम्प्रतिपन्नस्याभावात् ।

३६२. किञ्च धर्मिणो भिन्नत्वेन प्रतीतस्य प्रतियोगिता? अप्रतीतस्य वा?

359. "When it is intelligble that difference which exists and has been cognised as the very nature (of the substrate), is the qualification, what can the non-cognition of difference do"? If this be asked, no (says the Advaitin).

360. For, as between two trees at a distance, or as between milk and water, although difference exists in their nature and although (they are) manifested, there is not seen the cognition of being in conjunction etc.

361. If it be said that the non-cognition there is because of the presence of the defect *i.e.*, intermixture with things belonging to the same class, no (says the Advaitin), because of the non-existence of an admitted instance where relation of qualification and substrate is apprehended between existent differences and objects manifested as existent (svarūpeṇa).

362. Again does the counter-correlateness belong to what is cognised as different from the substrate, or to what is not cognised (as different)?

३६३. नाद्य: ; परस्पराश्रयतापातात् ; स्तम्भात्कुम्भभेदसिद्धौ कुम्भात् स्तम्भभेदसिद्धिरिति ।

३६४. न द्वितीय: ; आत्मनोऽपि प्रतियोगितापातात् ।

३६५. ननु निर्विकल्पकसंविदि भेदस्य भेदिनोश्च युगपदङ्गुलित्रयवदवभासे पुन: सविकल्पकधिया तद्विशेषणविशेष्यभावग्रहणोपपत्ते: कथमितरेतराश्रय इति चेन्न ।

३६६. निष्प्रतियोगिकभेदग्रहणस्यैवायोगात्; सर्वदा प्रतियोगिघटित एव तस्मिन्प्रमाणप्रसरात् ।

363. Not the first, because of the contingence of reciprocal dependence in that the difference of the pillar from the pot is established (only) when there is established the difference of the pot from the pillar.

364. Not the second, because of the contingence of (the substrate of difference) itself becoming the counter-correlate.

365. "Now when in the indeterminate cognition there is the simultaneous manifestation for the difference and the differents like (the cognition of) three fingers, since it is intelligible that, by the determinate cognition there is further the apprehension of the substrate-attribute relation between them, how is there (the defect of) reciprocal dependence?" If this be asked, no (says the siddhāntin).

366. For, the very cognition of difference, without the counter-correlate, is impossible, since always the means of valid knowledge functions in respect of it (the difference) only as bound with a counter-correlate.

३६७. किञ्च किमयं भेदो भिन्नमेव धर्मिणं परिरभते? उताभिन्नम्? नाद्यः; अनन्तभेदाभ्युपगमप्रसङ्गात्।

३६८. सन्त्वनन्तभेदाः; किं नश्छिन्नमिति चेन्न।

३६९. तेऽनन्ताः किं क्रमेण भेदा धर्मिणं परिरभन्ते? युगपद्वा?

३७०. नाद्यः; क्रमेण परिरभमाणानन्तभेदसम्बन्धाय धर्मिणोऽनादिनित्यतापातात्; प्रतिक्षणमेकैकभेदसम्बन्धेऽप्यनन्तक्षणवृत्तित्वस्य दुष्परिहरत्वात्।

367. Further, does this difference pertain to a substrate different from it, or that which is non-different from it? Not the first, because of the contingence of the acceptance of infinite differences.

368. If it be asked, "Let there be infinite differences; what is the harm to us (the Dvaitin)?" no (says the Advaitin).

369. Those infinite differences, do they pertain to the substrate (of difference) in sequence, or simultaneously?

370. Not the first, because of the contingence of the substrate becoming beginningless and eternal, for the sake of relation of the infinite differences that pertain to it in sequence. For, though at every single moment there is the relation (only) to a single difference, it is impossible to remedy the existence (of the substrate) for an infinity of moments.

३७१. न द्वितीयः; भिन्ने भेदस्थितिरिति पक्षक्षतेः; भेदसम्बन्धं विना भिन्नत्ववाचोयुक्तेरयुक्तत्वात्।

३७२. तत्सम्बन्धेनैव च भिन्नत्वे केन भेदेन विशिष्टे कस्य भेदस्य स्थितिरिति नियामकाभावात्तेषां कलहान्नैकोऽपि भेदो निविशेत्। तथापि चेच्छ्रद्धाजडोऽनन्तभेदानभ्युपैति, तदाभ्युपैतु यदि भेदपरम्परा संविदमध्यारोहेत।

३७३. न द्वितीयः; विरोधादेव, सर्वत्राप्यतिप्रसङ्गाच्च।

३७४. धर्मिणं परिरभ्यैव भेदो जायते; अतो नोक्तदोष इति चेत

371. Not the second; for there is destruction of the position that in the different there abides the difference. For, the verbal designation of difference in the absence of relation to difference does not stand to reason.

372. And if there be difference only because of relation to that (difference), since there is nothing to regulate as to for what there exists difference, (and) as qualified by what difference, there would be discord among those (differences); hence not even a single difference will enter into that (substrate). If still the dull man of faith admits infinite differences, let him admit them if the succession of differences get on to (his) consciousness.

373. Not the second, even because of contradiction, and because of the contingence of undue extension in respect of all things.

374. If it be said that the cognition of difference is born only as pertaining to the substrate and that

—मैवम्; धर्मिणा सहैव धर्मोत्पत्तेरनभ्युपगमात्। अभ्युपगमे चोत्पन्नं द्रव्यं क्षणमगुणं तिष्ठतीति कल्पनावैयर्थ्यात्; गुणानां द्रव्यजन्यत्वे धर्माणामपि तथात्वात्।

३७५. तस्मान्न भेदे प्रत्यक्षं प्रमाणम्। यदा तु भेदे न प्रत्यक्षं प्रमाणं तदा का वार्ता तत्पादोपजीविनो वराकस्यानुमानस्याप्रमाणतायाम्।

३७६. आत्मभेदस्तु न प्रमाणगन्धमनुभवति। न तावत्तत्र प्रत्यक्षं प्रमाणम्, परमात्मनोऽप्रत्यक्षत्वात्; प्रत्यक्षाप्रत्यक्षभेदस्य वायुवनस्पतिसंयोगवदप्रत्यक्षत्वात्।

therefore there is not the said defect, not so (says the Advaitin); for, the origination of attributes even along with the substrates is not accepted; because if it were accepted, the assumption that an originated substance exists for a moment without attributes would be futile, (and) because if qualities (like colour) are generated by substance (as material cause), the same is the case with attributes (like difference) too.

375. Therefore, in respect of difference, perception cannot be the means of valid knowledge. When perception cannot be the means of valid knowledge in respect of difference, why talk about invalidity of poor inference which lives at the feet of that (perception)?

376. As for differences of the self, that does not enjoy the slightest scent of any means of valid knowledge. Now, in respect of it (difference of the self) perception is not the means of valid knowledge, because the supreme self is not perceived; for the difference between the perceived and the unperceived is

३७७. आत्मा आत्मप्रतियोगिकभेदवान्, आत्मत्वादित्याद्यनु-मानस्य दृष्टान्तालाभदुष्टत्वात् ।

३७८. विप्रतिपन्नानि शरीराणि स्वसंख्यासंख्येयात्मवन्ति, शरीर-त्वादित्यस्यातीतानागतशरीरेषु व्यभिचारः । वर्त्तमानशरीरत्वहेतोर्योगिशरीरे व्यभिचारः ।

३७९. व्यवस्थानुपपत्तेश्च दुर्निरूपत्वेन भेदासाधकत्वम् । तथाहि—किं व्यवस्थापदेन धर्मभेदो विवक्षितः ? भिन्नाधिकरणधर्मभेदो वा ? विरुद्धत्वं वा ?

imperceptible like the conjunction that exists between the tree and the air.

377. (And it is so) because an inference like "the self has difference whose counter-correlate is the self, because it is the self," is defective, on account of the non-existence of an example.

378. In the inference "the bodies under dispute have the selves whose number is to be fixed by their own number, because of being a body", there is inconstancy (of the probans) in respect of the past and the future bodies. As for the nature of a present body being the probans, there is inconstancy in respect of the bodies of yogins (each of whom can animate more bodies than one).

379. And distinction (of experiences) being undemonstrable because of unintelligibility, it cannot establish difference. It is thus; what is it that is meant by the term "distinction?" Is it the difference between the attributes (in substrates) that are different,

३८०. नाद्यः; धर्मिभेदाभावेऽपि धर्मभेदोपपत्तेः। न द्वितीयः; परस्पराश्रयत्वात्।

३८१. न तृतीयः; "नाजात एकोऽन्यं हन्ति, नाप्यन्यमन्याधारः" इति न्यायेन सहावस्थानापेक्षणात्। तस्मान्न जडात्मनां भेदसिद्धिरिति।

३८२. अत्र प्रष्टव्यम्—किं भेदस्य प्रतीतिरेव निराक्रियते? उत तस्याः कारणजन्यता? निर्दोषकरणजन्यता वा?

or the difference between the attributes in different substrates, or is it contrariety?

380. Not the first, for, though there is non-existence of difference between substrates, difference among the attributes is intelligible. Not the second, because of the defect of reciprocal dependence.

381. Not the third, for on the principle that a thing which is not born does not kill another, nor does one (destroy) what is in a different substrate, there is need for the co-existence of the contraries (in the same locus). Therefore there is no establishment of difference in respect of the inert and in respect of souls.

XLI

382. Here it must be asked whether the cognition of difference itself is rejected, or its being originated by a cause, or its being originated by a non-defective instrument?

३८३. नाद्यः ; भेदस्य प्रतीतिमनुपजीव्य निराकर्तुमशक्यत्वात् । न द्वितीयः ; तत्किमजन्यतया स्यात्, अकारणजन्यतया अतत्कारणजन्यतया वा ?

३८४. नाद्यः ; अनभ्युपगमात् ; भेदप्रतीतेर्नित्यतापत्तेः स्वप्रातिकूल्याचरणप्रसङ्गाच्च ।

३८५. न द्वितीयः ; व्याघातात् ; तन्निवृत्तेरप्यकारणत्वापत्त्या प्रयत्नायोगाच्च ।

३८६. नापि तृतीयः ; तदुत्पादकस्यैव तत्कारणतया व्यवहारात् । न ह्यनुत्पादकादुत्पद्यते इति सम्भवति ; नाप्यन्योत्पादकात् ।

383. Not the first, because it is impossible to refute (difference) without basing (oneself) on the cognition of difference. Not the second. Would that be because of not being originated (at all), or because of not being originated by a cause, or because of not being originated by that cause?

384. Not the first, because of not being admitted, and because, on account of the contingence of the eternality of the cognition of difference, there is the contingence of the observance of what is opposed to yourselves (Advaitins).

385. Not the second, because of self-contradiction; and because, on account of the contingence of the removal of that (cognition) also being a non-cause, there is the impossibility of the effort (to attain release).

386. Nor even the third, since that which gives rise (to an object) is itself referred to as its cause. It cannot be that something is produced from what is not a producer or from the producer of another.

३८७. तृतीयेऽपि किं तर्केणैव सदोषत्वाध्यवसायः? अथ स्फुटतरबाधकवशात्?

३८८. नाद्यः; वेदान्तवाक्यवृत्तेरप्यविश्वसनीयतापातात्। दोषश्चात्राविद्यैव परस्येष्टा। सा च यदि वेदान्तानामपि मूलं तर्हि प्रत्यक्षे प्रद्वेषः किं निबन्धनः।

३८९. न द्वितीयः; निरवकाशस्य तस्यानुपलम्भात्।

३९०. कल्प्यमानमपि बाधकं किं भेदमेव गोचरयेत्? उताभेदम्? यद्वा यत्किञ्चित्, निरालम्बनस्यानुदयात्।

387. In the third case too, is the defectiveness ascertained by counter argument or because of some more prominent sublater?

388. Not the first, because of the contingence of the disbelief even in respect of psychosis generated by scriptural statements. And the defect admitted here by the opponents (Advaitins) is only nescience. And if this (defect) be at the root of Vedāntas too, then what is the cause of special a version to perception?

389. Not the second, because of the non-cognition of such (sublaters) having no scope (for being explained away).

390. Even what is assumed as sublater, does it have for its sphere difference alone, or non-difference or something else, since what is baseless cannot arise.

३९१. नाद्यः ; साधकत्वात् । द्वितीयेऽपि तदन्यः तद्विरोधी तदभावो वा नञर्थो वाच्यः ।

३९२. पक्षत्रयेऽपि दुष्परिहरो भेदः । भेदाभावग्राहिणापि प्रतियोगिविलक्षणतया स्वविषयो व्यवस्थाप्यः ।

३९३. नापि तृतीयः ; अविरोधादेव बाधकत्वायोगात् ।

३९४. किञ्च नायं भेद इति वा, नास्त्यत्र भेद इति वा, अन्यदेव भेदात्मना प्रत्यभादिति वा, बाधकज्ञानेन भवितव्यम् ; नेदं रजतं इत्यादिवत् ।

३९५. तदेतत्सर्वथा भेदावगाहीति कथं तत्परिपन्थिभावमाकल्पयेत् ।

391. Not the first, because it would establish (difference). In the second case too, the negative particle must be stated to mean what is different from it, or what is opposed to it, or what is its non-existence.

392. In all the three positions difference cannot be avoided. Even by one who apprehends the non-existence of difference there has to be established the content of his own (cognition) as different from the counter-correlate.

393. Not the third, since even because of non-conflict sublatership is not possible.

394. Again, "this is not difference"; "there is no difference here"; "some other thing itself is manifest as of the nature of difference": such must be the form of the sublating cognition, like the statement "this is not silver", etc.

395. Since this in every way comprehends difference, how can it take on a nature inimical thereto?

३९६. तस्मात्क्लृप्तविषयत्वान्नानवस्थादेरुत्थानम्। उत्थितस्य वा भवेदाभासत्वम्।

३९७. पारमार्थिकभेदानभ्युपगमेऽपि व्यावहारिकाङ्गीकारेण विकल्प्यनिराकरणोपपत्तिरिति चेन्न; स किं प्रत्यक्षाद्याकलितो वा अन्यो वा यो निराक्रियते।

३९८. आद्ये कथमङ्गीकृतस्य निराकरणम्? अन्यश्चेन्निषिध्यताम्; न नो हानिः।

३९९. न च प्रातिभासिक एवायं भेदः, अपसिद्धान्तापातात्।

396. Therefore, because of the content being determined (as validly known), there is no rise of (defects like) infinite regress, etc., or, in the case of such as arise, there could only be the nature of semblances.

397. If it be said that there is intelligibility of analysis and rejection, through the acceptance of the empirical reality (of difference) though there is the non-acceptance of the absolute reality of difference, no (says the siddhāntin). That (difference) which is rejected: is it what is established by perception, etc., or something else?

398. In the first case, how can there be the rejection of that which is accepted? If it is something else, let it be rejected; there is no loss for us (Dvaitins).

399. Nor is this difference merely 'apparent, because of the contingence of opposition to their (Advaitins) doctrine.

४००. नापि परप्रसिद्ध्या परबोधनम्, परस्य स्वक्रियास्वन्याय-विरुद्धविकल्पसाधुत्वाप्रसिद्ध्या बोधयितुमशक्यत्वात् ।

४०१. कथञ्चात्रापादनक्रमः ? यदि भेददर्शनं स्यात्, तदा अन्योन्याश्रयादिकं स्यात्; यदि भेददर्शनं वास्तवं स्यात्, तदा अन्योन्याश्रयादिकं स्यादिति वा ? यदि भेददर्शनं धर्म्यादिसापेक्षं स्यात्तर्हीति वा ?

४०२. नाद्यः; यदि भेददर्शनं न स्यात्तर्हि सकलव्यवहारविधुरः परः प्रसज्यतेति प्रतितर्कपराहतत्वात् ।

400. Nor is it instruction of the opponent through what is established for the opponent; for there is no possibility of teaching the opponent because of the soundness of the alternatives not being established (for him) in as much as they are unreasonable and conflict with ones own actions.

401. What is the form of deduction (of the defect) here? Is it that if there be the cognition of difference, then, there would be (defects like) reciprocal dependence, etc., or that if the cognition of difference be true, there would be (defects like) reciprocal dependence, etc., or that if the cognition of difference be dependent on the (cognition of) the substrate, etc., then, (there would be the defect of reciprocal dependence)?

402. Not the first, for, there is the refutation by the following counter argument, against it, "If there were no cognition of difference, then there is the contingence of the opponent being devoid of all empirical usage."

४०३. न द्वितीयः; व्याप्तिवैकल्यात्। तृतीयेऽपि सापेक्षतामात्रं निवर्त्तताम्; दर्शनस्य किमायातम्?

४०४. प्रकारान्तरासम्भवात् स्वयमपि निवर्त्तते इति चेन्न; प्रकारान्तरेण निर्वाहकल्पनस्य शक्यत्वेन प्रतीतेरपह्नवायोगात्। अन्यथा स्वाभिलषितस्याप्यभेदस्यासिद्धेरुक्तत्वात्।

४०५. इयञ्चात्र दर्शनस्थितिः—न भेदो युगधर्मः, किन्त्वेकस्य धर्मोऽपरेण निरूप्यः।

403. Not the second, because of the defect in respect of the pervasion (which is not established, there being no example). In the third case also let the dependence alone disappear; what (defect) occurs to the cognition (of difference)?

404. If it be said that, because of the non-existence of another mode (of arising) that (cognition of difference) too disappears, no (says the Advaitin), because, it being possible to assume another mode of explanation, the denial of the cognition (of difference) is not reasonable; for it has been said that otherwise even the non-difference cherished by (the opponent) himself would be non-established.

XLII

405. And this is the position of the system in this matter. Difference is not a common attribute. It is rather the attribute of one (object) indicated by another.

४०६. इमौ भिन्नावित्यत्रापि स्तम्भात्कुम्भस्य भेदः, कुम्भात्स्तम्भस्य भेद इत्येवार्थः ।

४०७. अनयोर्भेद इति तूभयधार्मिकं भेदद्वयमेव । एकवचनं तु—अनयोः स्वरूपम्—इतिवत् ।

४०८. स च भेदो धर्मिणस्स्वरूपमेव । अन्यथा स्वरूपं प्रतीयमानं सर्वात्मना प्रतीयेत । तथा चात्मन्यपि घटोऽहमिति प्रतीतिप्रसङ्गः । न हि दृष्टपदार्थस्य पुरुषस्य वस्त्वन्तरात्तस्य भेदे संशयः क्वचिद्दृष्टः ।

४०९. न च सर्वतो व्यावृत्त्यनुभवे सार्वज्ञ्यापत्तिदोषः, सामान्यतः सर्वस्य साक्षिसिद्धत्वाङ्गीकाराच्च ।

406. Even in (the statement) "these two are different" the meaning is only "the pillar is different from the pot and the pot is different from pillar."

407. As for (the statement) "the difference between the two" (it denotes) only two differences present in the two substrates. The singular number is as in (the usage) "the existence (or nature—savarūpa) of the two".

408. And this difference is the very nature of the substrate. Otherwise a nature when cognised will be cognised as of the nature of all (things). And then there is the contingence of the cognition "I am a pot", even in respect of the self. Indeed, for the individual who has cognised an object, there is nowhere seen any doubt regarding its difference from the other object.

409. Nor is there the defect that if there be the experience of difference from all (others), there is the

४१०. अन्यथा सार्वत्रिकव्याप्तिपरिज्ञानासम्भवेन सर्वानुमानतर्कोच्छेदप्रसङ्गः ।

४११. न च विशेषज्ञानापेक्षा, भेदस्वरूपमात्रप्रतीतेस्तदनपेक्षणात् ।

४१२. न च संशयाभावप्रसङ्गः, कुतश्चिद्व्यावृत्तस्य वस्तुनः प्रतीतावपि व्यावृत्तिविशेषाग्रहणवशादेव संशयोत्पत्तेः । अन्यथा सर्वकोट्यवलम्बी संशयः स्यात् ।

contingence of omniscience, because it is admitted that all objects are in their general nature established by witness (consciousness).

410. Otherwise, because of the impossibility of the proper cognition of pervation everywhere, there is the contingence of the destruction of all inferences and counter-arguments.

411. And there is no need for knowledge of (all things) in their particularity; for that is not necessary for the cognition of the mere existence (svarūpa) of the difference.

412. Nor is there the contingence of the non-existence of doubt. For, though there is the cognition of a thing as different from some other, even because of the non-apprehension of the particular difference, there is intelligibility of doubt; otherwise, (if difference were not at all apprehended) doubt would be in respect of all possibilities (*i.e.*, in respect of a post, the doubt would be as to difference not merely from man, etc., but also from cloth, etc.)

४१३. स्वरूपत्वेन च भेदस्यानेकप्रतीत्यभावान्नान्योन्याश्रयादेरवकाशः। अस्ति तावत्, अस्तीदम्—इत्यत्र वर्तमानकालो वस्तुना सहैवानुभूयते साक्षिणेति।

४१४. तदुक्तम्—

तदेतदिति सर्वञ्च दृश्यं वा स्मृतिगोचरम्।
साक्षिसिद्धेन कालेन खचितं ह्येव वर्तते॥ इति।

४१५. न ह्यानुमानिकः कालः; कालसिद्ध्यसिद्ध्योः सिद्धसाधनाश्रयासिद्धिभ्यां तमेव पक्षीकृत्यानुमानस्यानुत्थानात्।

XLIII

413. Since, difference being the very nature of the substrate, there is not more than one cognition (to apprehend the thing and its difference) there is no occasion for (defects like) reciprocal dependence, etc. (In the cognitions) "now, there is" (and) "this is" the present time (indicated by the word is) is certainly experienced together with the object (brought in) by the witness (consciousness).

414. That has been said (by S'rī Madhva):

> (Things) cognised as 'that' (related to past time) and recollected as 'this' (related to preset time), all of them exist only as mixed with time, that is established by witness (consciousness.)

415. Nor is time established by inference; for inference cannot arise with that (time) itself as the

४१६. नापि तत्सम्बन्धिनः कस्यचित्पक्षीकारेणानुमानप्रवृत्तिः ; कालवृत्तिमन्तरेण तेन साहचर्यस्मरणाद्यसम्भवात् ।

४१७. अत्र केचिदाहुः—बहुतरणिपरिस्पन्दान्तरितजन्मत्वं परत्वम्। अल्पतरसूर्यसञ्चारान्तरितजनिमत्वं चापरत्वम् । एकतपनप्रचारविशिष्टत्वं यौगपद्यम् । अनेकतद्विशिष्टत्वमयौगपद्यम् । बहुतपनक्रियाविशिष्टत्वमक्षिप्रत्वम् । कतिपयक्रियाविशिष्टत्वं क्षिप्रत्वम् । तत्प्रत्ययैरनुमेयः कालः ।

subject (pakṣa), because whether it (time) is (already) established or non-established there are (respectively the defects of) the establishment of the established and the non-establishment of the locus (of the inference, *i.e.*, the subject).

416. Nor is there the possibility of an inference having for its subject something related to that (time); for, in the absence of a psychosis (in respect) of time, it is not possible to have recollection of concomitance (*i.e.*, pervasion) etc. with that (time).

417. Here, some (the Logicians) say (thus); priority consists in having a birth remote (from present) by many circuits of the sun, and posteriority consists in having a birth remote by fewer circuits of the sun; contemporaneity consists in being qualified by the same locomotion of the sun; non-contemporaneity consists in being qualified by different such (locomotions of the sun); non-quickness consists in being qualified by many acts (of locomotion) of the sun; quickness consists in being qualified by a few (such) acts; time is what is inferred through these cognitions. Indeed

तरणिपरिस्पन्दा हि पदार्थसार्थे विशिष्टप्रत्ययहेतुतया स्वप्रत्यासत्तिमपेक्षन्ते, विशिष्टव्यवहारजनकत्वात्, चन्दनसौरभवत् ।

४१८. स च सम्बन्धः परम्परया वाच्यः साक्षादसम्भवात्, पटविशेषणस्येव नीलिम्नः ।

४१९. अतः पदार्थानां तपनपरिस्पन्दैः संयुक्तसंयोगिसमवायात्मके सम्बन्धे यन्निमित्तं द्रव्यं स काल इति ।

४२०. तदसत्; वाच्यवाचकादिवत्स्वभावप्रत्यासत्त्यैव विशिष्टप्रतीत्युपपत्तेः । अन्यथा युगपदुत्पन्नाभावादिषु यौगपद्यव्यवहारो न स्यात् ।

the circuits of the sun, being the cause of a cognition as qualified, require a connection of their selves with the assemblage of objects, because they give rise to the empirical usage (of the objects) as qualified (as prior, posterior, etc.), like the scent of the sandal-wood.

418. And this relation must be said to be indirect, since the direct (relation) is impossible, as in the case of blueness, as an attribute of a cloth.

419. Therefore, that substance which is the (mediating) cause in (establishing) the relation of the nature of inherence in that which is conjoined to what is in conjunction, between objects and the movements of the sun, that is time.

420. That is unsound; for there is intelligibility for the cognition of the qualified even through a natural relation, as in the relation between word and the word-sense. Otherwise, there would be no empirical usage of simultaneity in respect of non-existence, (cognitions) etc., that arise simultaneously.

४२१. एवं परापरव्यवहारोऽपि । दिश एव कल्प्यतामुभयविध-परापरत्वव्यवहारनिर्वाहकत्वम् । अप्रसिद्धकालकल्पनात्प्रसिद्धस्यैवोपनायकता-कल्पनस्य लघुत्वात् ।

४२२. शब्दाश्रयतया गगनानुमाने च जातिबधिरमूकादेर्गगना-निश्चयात्सञ्चार एव कुण्ठितः स्यात् । अरूपिद्रव्येषु चक्षुर्व्यापारायोगात् ।

४२३. कूपोऽयम्, रन्ध्रमेतत्—इत्यादौ चक्षुर्व्यापारस्यावरणा-भावविषयतयाप्युपपत्तेः ।

421. So also the usage in respect of priority and posteriority. Let there be assumed of space itself the capacity to account for the two-fold usage of priority and posteriority; for instead of assuming an unknown time, the assumption of mediatorship for the known space is more in accordance with the principle of parsimony.

422. And in the inference of ether as the substrate of sound, since there is no ascertainment of (such) ether for those congenitally deaf or dumb, movement itself (dependent on cognition of ether) would be difficult. (But this is not so. Hence space too must be witness-established. Nor may it be said space is directly visible). For it is impossible for the eye to function in respect of colourless substances (like ether).

423. In "this is well", "this is a hole", etc., (where there is apparent visible cognition of ether) there is intelligibility for the functioning of the eye, even through (that activity) relating to the non-existence of obstruction.

४२४. न चैवमाकाशस्यैवापह्नवः, अत्रावरणाभाव इति तदाश्रयतया झडित्येव स्फुरणात्। न चैवं गगने व्यवहारः। कचित्—इह गगनम्—इति व्यवहारस्तु मूर्त्तवस्तुसम्बन्धवशाद्वा प्रदेशनिष्ठतया वा निर्वहति।

४२५. शब्दो विभुगुणो न भवति, बाह्येन्द्रियग्राह्यगुणत्वादिति किं नानुमीयते? स्पर्शो न पृथिव्यादिगुणः, नीरूपेन्द्रियग्राह्यत्वादिति द्रव्यान्तरं वा किमिति न लभ्यते।

४२६. अत आकाशकालदिगात्ममनांसि सुखदुःखेच्छादयश्च सा-

424. Nor is thus (the existence of) ether itself denied; for in the form "here is no obstruction" it (ether) is immediately cognised as the substrate of that. And there is not thus such empirical usage (like "here is ether") in respect of ether. As, however, for the usage sometimes (in the form) "here is ether", that is explained as due either to being related to some corporeal substance (like, pot, room, etc.) or to referring to a (particular) locality (as content).

425. Why is there not inferred that sound is not the quality of what is all-pervasive, because it is an attribute cognised by an external sense-organ (like colour)? (Likewise), why is there not established some other substance (for touch etc.) since touch is not an attribute of earth, etc., because it is cognised by a sense-organ that has no colour (like sound or cognition).

426. Therefore ether, time, space, self, mind, pleasure, pain, desire etc., are directly the spheres of

क्षात्साक्षिगोचराः । अन्ये तु पदार्थाः यथायथमिन्द्रियलिङ्गागमगम्या इत्याचार्यसिद्धान्तः ।

४२७. प्रमाणानां प्रामाण्यनिर्वाहकत्वेन चापेक्षणीयः साक्षी । तद्धि याथार्थ्यलक्षणं किमदुष्टकरणजन्यत्वेनावसेयम्, दुष्टकरणाजन्यत्वेन वा? अथ प्रवृत्तिसामर्थ्येन, यद्वा ज्ञानान्तरसंवादेन? किं वा विसंवादाभावेन? आहोस्वित्स्वतः?

४२८. नाद्यः; तस्यैव दुरवधारणत्वात् । ज्ञानयाथार्थ्येन तन्निश्चये परस्पराश्रयापातः ।

the witness (consciousness). Other objects, however, are respectively cognised by the appropriate means of valid knowledge of sense-organ, inference and verbal testimony; this is the final position of the Teacher.

XLIV

427. And the witness (consciousness) has to be sought as accounting for the validity of the means of valid knowledge. Indeed, that (validity) consisting in correspondence to the object, is it to be ascertained through (1) being generated by non-defective instruments, or (2) not being generated by defective instruments, or (3) successful nature of activity, or (4) the agreement with another cognition, or (5) the absence or disagreement (with another knowledge), or (6) intrinsically?

428. Not the first, because that (being generated by non-defective instrument) itself is difficult to ascertain. In ascertaining (it) through the validity of cognition

४२९. अत एव न द्वितीयः। नापि तृतीयः, सर्वत्र ज्ञाने तदभावात्।

४३०. चतुर्थस्तु, सुखादिज्ञानेष्वसम्भावितः। ज्ञानमात्रसंवादेन च प्रामाण्याभ्युपगमे धारावाहिकविभ्रमो नाम न स्यात्। यथार्थज्ञानसंवादाभ्युपगमे च तस्यापि याथार्थ्यावधारणायामनवस्था स्यात्।

४३१. न पञ्चमः; अनुपसञ्जातबाधभ्रमेष्वपि प्रामाण्यनिश्चयापातात्, पुरुषदेशकालविशेषविकल्पानुपपत्तेश्च।

there is the contingence of (the defect of) reciprocal dependence.

429. For the same reason (it can) not (be) the second. Nor even the third, because that does not exist in all cognitions.

430. As for the fourth however, it is not possible in respect of the cognition of pleasure, etc. And if validity be accepted because of the agreement with cognition as such (not valid cognition), there would not be what is called a continuous stream of delusive cognitions. And if what is accepted be agreement with a valid cognition, in ascertaining the validity of that (cognition) too, there would be (the defect of) infinite regress.

431. Not the fifth, because there is the contingence of ascertainment of validity even in respect of delusions for which a sublation has not yet arisen, and because there is unintelligibility on the analysis (of the alternatives in respect) of such details as person, place, time, etc.

४३२. न षष्ठः; अनात्मरूपेषु मनोवृत्तिज्ञानेषु स्वयंप्रकाशत्वासम्भवात्।

४३३. वेदवाक्याद्बाह्यस्योत्पन्ने ज्ञाने तत्प्रामाण्यं तेनैव स्फुरति न वा?

४३४. आद्ये, न तन्निराकुर्यात्। द्वितीये, कथं स्वतस्त्वसिद्धिः। अपौरुषेयत्वादियुक्तिभिः कथं वा परः पश्चात्प्रतिबोध्यते।

४३५. न च ज्ञानतत्प्रामाण्ययोः सहैवानुमानमिति पक्षः, अनुमेयत्वे मानाभावात्, व्यवहारस्य त्वन्यथाप्युपपत्तेः, अपरोक्षानुभवविरोधाच्च।

432. Not the sixth; for self-luminosity is not possible in respect of cognitions which are psychoses of the mind (manas) and are of the nature of not-self.

433. In the cognition generated by scriptural statements in the mind of one who stands outside (the belief in scriptural statements), is its validity manifested by itself or not?

434. In the first case, it should not have been rejected (by him). In the second case, how is (its) intrinsic nature established? And how can it be that subsequently the opponent is enlightened with (the help of) such probans as "being (of) superhuman (composition)" etc.?

435. Nor (can) the view (be held) that of cognition and its validity there is inference even together, since in respect of (validity) being inferred there is no authority, in as much as, empirical usage is intelligible even otherwise, and since there is conflict with the direct experience.

४३६. ज्ञानं हि ज्ञाततया व्यवहारेण वा कार्येणानुमेयम्। न च तत्प्रामाण्याविनाभावि; शुक्तिरूप्यादौ व्यभिचारात्।

४३७. बाह्यागमज्ञानानामपि प्रामाण्यानुमानप्रसङ्गः। प्रसक्तमप्यपोह्यते इति चेत्—तर्ह्यपवादनिरासाय परीक्षापेक्षायां यौगपद्यभङ्गात्कुतो ज्ञानग्राहकमात्रग्राह्यत्वम्। तस्माज्ज्ञानग्राहकेणैव साक्षिणा तत्प्रामाण्याध्यवसायः।

४३८. स च ज्ञानं गृह्णन् दोषं चेत् प्रमाणम्, न चेदन्यथा—इत्येव व्यवस्थया गृह्णाति। तथा च नारोपितज्ञानप्रामाण्यग्रहणप्रसङ्गः।

436. Cognition indeed would have to be inferred from the effect *i.e.*, cognisedness or empirical usage. And that (effect) is not non-existent without validity, because of inconstancy in the case of shell-silver etc.

437. There is the contingence of the inference of validity even in respect of cognitions from the scriptures by outsiders (those who do not believe in vedas). If it be said that (such validity) though contingent is denied, then, verification being needed to refute exceptions (to validity), the stimultaneity (of cognition and validity) fails; whence then is the (possibility of validity) being apprehended by that much alone which apprehends the cognition? Therefore only by the witness (consciousness) which apprehends the cognition is its validity ascertained.

XLV

438. And that (witness-consciousness) in apprehending cognition, apprehends it only as thus distinct, "if non-defective, then valid; if not, it is otherwise."

४३९. यदा त्वर्थित्वेन प्रामाण्यं निश्चिचीषति, तदा सजातीय-विजातीयसंवादविसंवादभावाभावलक्षणया परीक्षया दोषाभावं निश्चित्य प्रामाण्यमवधारयति । दोषदर्शने त्वप्रामाण्यम् ।

४४०. न च परीक्षायां परीक्षान्तरापेक्षायामनवस्था । नापि स्व-परीक्षापेक्षा । साक्षिरूपस्यानुभवस्य स्वप्रकाशात्मस्वरूपत्वाभ्युपगमान्न तत्र परीक्षापेक्षा ।

४४१. मामहं जानामीत्यनुभवाद्विशेषबलाच्च न कर्तृकर्मभाव-विरोधः ।

And thus there is not the contingence of the cognition of validity in respect of a superimposed cognition.

439. However, for any one seeking (a successful result) there is desire to ascertain validity, then (such a person) after ascertaining non-existence of defect through verification consisting in the existence and non-existence of aggreement and disagreement with what are of the same class or are of a different class, concludes the validity; but, on the cognition of defect, (he concludes) invalidity.

440. Nor through dependence for (this) verification on another verification is there (the defect of) infinite regress. Neither in respect of (witness-consciousness) itself is there need for verification. Since the experience of the nature of the witness is admitted to be the very nature of the self-luminous self, there is not in respect of that, the dependence on verification.

441. There is no conflict between the relation of agent and object (in one and the same), because of

४४२. नापि स्वानुभूतेषु परीक्षाकांक्षा ; तस्यादोषतया संशयानवकाशात् ।

४४३. तदुक्तम्—

> सुदृढो निर्णयो यत्र ज्ञेयं तत्साक्षिदर्शनम् ।
> न परीक्षानवस्था स्यात्साक्षिसिद्धे त्वसंशयात् ॥ इति ।
> यत्कचिद्व्यभिचारि स्याद्दर्शनं मानसं हि तत् । इति च ।

४४४. तथाहि—अस्त्यत्र पानीयमिति श्रुतवतः तत्प्रामाण्ये सन्दि-

the experience "I know myself" and on the strength of (the category) particularity (*i.e.*, the specific capacity of entities—vis'eṣa).

442. Nor is there the need for verification in respect of what are experienced by (the witness) itself; for, that (witness-consciousness) being non-defective, there is no scope for doubt.

443. That is stated:

> "where there is very firm certainty, that should be known to be witness-cognition; there would be no infinite regress through verification, because there is no doubt in respect of whatever is established by the witness (consciousness),"

and

> "where in some cases that (the above principle) is inconstant that, indeed, is a mental cognition (due to a psychosis)".

444. It is thus: for him who, having heard that there is (water) to drink here, doubts the validity of

हानस्य वायुविशेषादिभिरनुमानमपि समुदेति । तत्रापि साशङ्कश्चेच्चक्षुषैव निश्चिनोति ।

४४५. प्रत्यासन्नश्च सलिलपानानन्तरमुदन्याभावनिमित्तं दुःखाभावं सुखञ्च साक्षादेव साक्षिणानुभवन्न तत्र संशेते ।

४४६. सुखदुखेच्छातदभावादिषु साक्षिसिद्धेषु कचिदन्यथाभावस्यानुपलम्भात् ।

४४७. अन्यथा सर्वत्र संशयानपगमात्सर्वव्यवहारलोपप्रसङ्गः ।

that (statement), there arises inference also through a particular (*i.e.* cold) breeze, etc. If doubtful even in that case, he (then) makes certain even with the sense of sight.

445. And he who has gone near it (water) and after drinking the water, experiencing directly through the witness (consciousness) the pleasure and the absence of pain, due to the non-existence of thirst, has no doubt in respect of these.

446. For there is not anywhere the cognition as being otherwise (than they are) in respect of what are established by the witness (consciousness) such as pleasure, pain, desire and their (respective) non-existences.

447. Otherwise, because of the non-removal of doubt in every case, there is the contingence of the failure of all empirical usage.

४४८. मानसवृत्तिषु पुनरनादौ संसारे द्वयीं गतिमनुसन्दधत्साक्षी सहसैव प्रमाणमेतदिति न निश्चेतुं प्रभवति । किन्तु दोषाभावनिश्चयद्वारैव ।

४४९. दोषाभावं च न स्वयमेवावधारयितुमीष्टे ; अपि तु परीक्षा-सहकृत एव । परीक्षाया अपि यावत्स्वविषयेषु सुखादिषु पर्यवसानं तावत्प-रीक्षान्तरमनुसरति ।

४५०. न हि स्वात्मनि कदाप्यन्यथाभावः, येन परीक्षानवस्था स्यात् ।

४५१. न चैवं परतस्त्वापत्तिः, परीक्षायाः प्रतिबन्धकदोषशङ्का-निरसने परिक्षीणत्वात् ।

448. In respect of mental psychoses however, the witness recollecting the two ways (validity as well as invalidity) in this beginningless world (samsāra) is not capable of ascertaining at once, " this is valid ". But (it does so) only through the ascertainment of the non-existence of defect.

449. And a non-existence of defect it is able to ascertain, not of itself, but only as aided by verification. And till there is culmination of the verifications in pleasure, etc., which are the contents of (the witness) itself, it goes after another verification.

450. There is never indeed any (cognition as) being otherwise in respect of that (witness-consciousness) itself, in which case there would be infinite regress of verifications.

451. Nor is there thus the contigence of extrinsic nature (for validity), for verification becomes obsolete

४५२. न हि गोक्षुरकापसरणसापेक्षत्वेन गजस्य गमनशक्तिः परतन्त्रा ।

४५३. न चैवमप्रामाण्यस्यापि स्वतस्त्वापत्तिः । विसंवादानुसन्धानवतामेवाप्रामाण्यज्ञप्तिरित्यव्यभिचरितानन्यथासिद्धान्वयव्यतिरेकवशादनुमेयत्वाध्यवसायात् ।

४५४. प्रामाण्यनिश्चये तु प्रतिबन्धकनिवर्तकतया क्वचिदेव परीक्षापेक्षेति वैषम्यम् । न चाप्रामाण्यं क्वापि निरपेक्षेण साक्षिणा निश्चितचरम्, येन प्रतिबन्धकनिवर्तकतां तस्यां प्रतीमः ।

(in function) with the refutation of the doubt as to obstructing defect.

452. Because of dependence on the removal of the thorn, the elephant's capacity for motion is not indeed dependent on something else.

453. Nor is there thus the contigence of intrinsic nature for invalidity too. For, the cognition of invalidity is only for those men who recollect disagreement; because of this concomitance and non-concomitance which are non-inconstant and not accounted for otherwise it is concluded that (invalidity) is (only) inferrable.

454. In respect of the ascertainment of validity, however, there is only in some cases the dependence on verification as removing obstructions; hence there is disparity (betwen the two). And nowhere previously has invalidity been ascertained by the witness (consciousness) without dependence (on verification), in which case we would cognise there (too) the removal of obstruction.

४५५. दोषाभावान्वयव्यतिरेकनियमांत्प्रामाण्यस्य परतस्त्वं किं न स्यादिति चेन्न; यादृच्छिकसंवादिषु प्रामाण्येऽपि दोषाभावाभावेन कारणत्वभङ्गात् ।

४५६. वेत्रबीजस्य स्वाङ्कुरजननशक्तेर्दाहाभावप्रयुक्ततापत्तिः । तथा च न क्वाप्युत्सर्गापवादौ स्यातामिति ।

४५७. कथञ्चित्सापेक्षत्वेन परतस्त्वे साक्षिणः साक्षात्स्वतःप्रामाण्यम्, तदन्यस्यासाक्षादिति व्यवस्था स्यात् ।

455. It if be asked why there should not be extrinsic nature for validity (too) because of regulation by concomitance and non-concomitance with non-existence of defect, no (says the siddhāntin). For though there is validity in cases of accidental agreement, since there is the non-existence of the non-existence of defect, there is failure of causality (for the said non-existence).

456. There is the contingence of the potency of the cane (vetra) seed to give rise to its own sprout, being due to the non-existence of fire. And thus there would nowhere be a general law and the exceptions.

XLVI

457. If somehow there be extrinsic nature on account of dependence, there could be a distinction that the self-validity for that witness (consciousness) is direct, and for what is other than that (witness-consciousness) it is indirect.

४५८. तस्मात्सुषुप्तावपि सुखानुभवादिविशेषणतया प्रतीयमानः कालः साक्षिणैवेक्षणीयः ।

४५९. तथा चात्र प्रयोगः—कालो बाह्यप्रत्यक्षाद्यतिरिक्तप्रमाण-विषयः, असत्स्वपि तेषु प्रतीयमानत्वात् ; यो यस्मिन्नसति प्रतीयते स तद्व्य-तिरिक्तप्रमाणविषयः, यथा सति चक्षुषि प्रतीयमानो गन्ध इति ।

४६०. तेन च कालेन सर्वं विशिष्टमेवानुभूयते इति सर्वाधारतया-स्थेयम् । अस्त्यासीद्भविष्यतीति वा प्रतीतिमपहाय पदार्थप्रतीतेरौदासीन्येना-ननुभवात् ।

458. Therefore, even in sleep, time, cognised as the qualification of the experience of pleasure etc., is to be cognised only by the witness-consciousness.

459. And thus the inference here is: "Time is the object of a means of valid knowledge, other than external perception, etc., because of being cognised even where they (other means of valid knowledge) are non-existent; that which is cognised in the absence of some (means of valid knowledge) is the content of a means of valid knowledge other than that, like smell that is cognised in the absence of the sense of sight.

XLVII

460. Since everything is experienced only as qualified by such time (as established by the witness-consciousness) it (time) is to be admitted as the substrate of all. For, there is no experience of a

४६१. तद्वदेव युगपत्प्रतीतयोर्धर्मिप्रतियोगिभावेन भेदप्रतीत्युपपत्तेरपि नान्योन्याश्रयाद्यापातः ।

४६२. अत एव परस्परभेदप्रतीतेरपि तत्तत्प्रत्ययापृथग्भावान्नान्योन्यापेक्षा ।

४६३. परमात्मतदितरभेदोऽपि तत्तत्स्वरूपग्राहकप्रमाणावसेय इति नोक्तदोषावकाशः । न हि धर्मिप्रतियोगिभेदप्रत्ययानां क्रमभावे मानं पश्यामः ।

neutral cognition of objects without the cognition "is", "was", or "will be".

461. Even likewise, there is no contingence of (the defect of) reciprocal dependence etc., even because of the intelligibility of the cognition of difference as substrate and counter-correlate, in the case of a pair simultaneously cognised.

462. For the same reason even in the case of the cognition of reciprocal difference, since each (such cognition) is inseparable from the corresponding cognition (of the substrate or the counter-correlate) there is no mutual dependence.

XLVIII

463. There is no room for the adduced defect, since even the difference between the supreme self and other things has to be determined by the means of valid knowledge apprehending the respective entities. We see indeed no authority for a relation of sequence among the cognitions of the substrate, the counter-correlate and the difference.

४६४. जीवब्रह्मैक्यवदेव स्वरूपयोः सापेक्षनिरपेक्षत्वे, कचित्प्रतीताप्रतीतत्वे अस्येदमिति सम्बन्धितयावभासोऽपर्यायशब्दवाच्यत्वमित्यादिवैचित्र्यं द्रष्टव्यम् ।

४६५. व्यपदेशमात्रमत्रेति चेत् कोऽर्थः? किं परमार्थेन स्वरूपं नाम बाधितम्, ऐक्यं वा, तत्सम्बन्धो वा, व्यवहारो वा तन्निमित्तं वा?

४६६. नाद्यः; निराश्रयस्यैक्यस्यानिर्वाहात् । निर्वाहे वा ब्रह्मैक्यवादस्तुच्छाद्वैते पर्यवस्येत् ।

464. Like the identity of the individual self and Brahman, there is to be noted variety for one's own nature (as between two things) such as, dependence and non-dependence, cognisedness and non-cognisedness in some place, manifestation in the relation (of the form) "of this it is", and denotation by non-synonymous words and others.

465. If it be said that it is a mere verbal statement, "what does it mean?" (asks the siddhāntin). Is it that what is called existence is sublated in reality, or identity, or its relation, or empirical usage, or its cause?

466. Not the first, because of the impossibility of maintaining identity devoid of a substrate. Or if maintained, the doctrine of the identity of the Brahman with the (individual) self would culminate in the non-dualism of nullity.

४६७. न द्वितीयः; भेदोन्मज्जनप्रसङ्गात्; न ह्युभयोदासीनतत्त्वसिद्धिः; उभयात्मकवस्तुवत्तस्यापि व्याहतत्वात्।

४६८. न तृतीयः; ऐक्यस्यान्यसम्बन्धितापातात्। मेरुमन्दरादिवत्स्वातन्त्र्येण प्रतीतिप्रसङ्गाच्च।

४६९. नापि तुरीयः; अर्थबाधमन्तरेण व्यवहारबाधस्यासिद्धेः; आत्मैक्यस्य बाधितत्वे तत्त्वमसीति वाक्यस्यातत्त्वावेदकत्वापातात्।

४७०. न च पञ्चमः; नैमित्तिकदर्शनादेव निमित्तकल्पनासौलभ्यात्। अन्यथात्मैक्यपदयोः पर्यायताप्रसङ्गः।

467. Not the second, because of the contingence of difference rising up. Nor is there, indeed, the establishment of a reality indifferent to either, because that too is contradicted, like the thing which is of the nature of both.

468. Not the third, since there is the contingence of identity being related to something else, and since there is (also) the contingence of the independent cognition (in respect of it) as in the case of the mountains, Meru and Mandara.

469. Nor the fourth, since there is no establishment of the sublation of empirical usage without the sublation of the object; for if the identity of the self be sublated, then for the text "That thou art", there is the contingence of making known the unreal.

470. Nor the fifth, because of ease in postulating the cause even from the cognition of the caused.

४७१. तच्च निमित्तं भेदोऽत्र बाधित इति चेत्तर्हि तत्प्रतिनिधिः स्वनिर्वाहको विशेषो नाम पदार्थशक्तिरभिषिच्यताम् ।

४७२. न चैवमतिप्रसङ्गः, मुख्यनिमित्तस्यान्यत्र सम्भवेऽन्यस्य कल्पनायोगात् ।

४७३. निर्भेदे वस्तुनि भेदवन्निर्विशेषे तस्मिन्विशेषोऽपि व्याहत इति चेन्न; निर्विशेषत्वविशेषवदुपपत्तेः । स च यदि विरोधात्त्यज्येत, तर्हि सुतरां सविशेषतासिद्धिः ।

Otherwise there is the contingence of the terms "self" and "identity" becoming synonymous.

XLIX

471. If it be said that that cause, namely, difference, is sublated here, then (the siddhāntin says) let there be installed as its substitute a potency of things called particularity (vis'eṣa) which can account for itself.

472. And there is not thus (the defect) of undue extension. When there is the possibility of the principal cause (*viz.* difference) in other cases (pot, cloth etc.) it is not proper to assume some other (like vis'eṣa).

473. If it be said that just like difference in an object devoid of difference, particularity too in an object devoid of particularity is contradicted, no (says the siddhāntin); for it is intelligible like the particularity of being devoid of particularity. And if that

४७४. तदुक्तमाचार्यैः—

> भेदे हीने त्वपर्यायशब्दान्तरनियामकः ।
> विशेषो नाम कथितः सोऽस्ति वस्तुष्वशेषतः ॥ इति ।

४७५. स्वरूपव्यतिरिक्तं भेदमभ्युपगच्छतामपि स्वरूपभेदयोर्भेदस्य स्वनिर्वाहकता सिद्धा । तैरपि निर्वाह्यनिर्वाहकनिर्वहणादिरूपवैचित्र्यमेकस्यैव भेदस्याङ्गीकृतं भवेत्, अन्यथानवस्थानात् । ततो वरं पदार्थस्यैव विचित्र-शक्तिस्वीकार इति ।

(particularity) be given up because of contradiction, then all the easier is the establishment of the possession of particularity.

474. That has been said by the Teacher:

> "But where there is no difference (the category) called particularity is declared (to exist) as the regulator of (the use of) another non-synonymous word; that exists in all things without exception".

475. Even for those who accept the difference as other than one's own nature, there is established the self-explanatory nature of the difference between one's own nature and difference. By them too comes to be accepted in respect of one and the same difference such a variety of characteristics as being that which is explained, that which explains and explanation, as otherwise there is (the defect of) infinite regress. Better

४७६. अन्यैरपि समवायस्याश्रितत्वादिव्यवहारे गतिरियमेवानुसरणीया ।

४७७. तस्माद् ब्रह्मस्वरूपावगाहि "विज्ञानमानन्दं ब्रह्म" इत्यादिवाक्यसमानयोगक्षेमतया भेदप्रपञ्चमध्यक्षवतः प्रत्यक्षस्य दुराक्षेपैर्नाधिक्षेपः ।

४७८. शरीरत्वहेतुरपि परस्परानुसंहितभोगायतनत्वेन विवक्षित इति न तत्रापि दोषः । नापि दृष्टान्तालाभः । योगिशरीराणां व्यतिरेकिदृष्टान्ततासम्भवात् ।

than that is it to accept the variety of potency for the thing itself.

476. By others also, in respect of empirical usage as to inherence being located (in the substrate) and so on, this method (of explanation) alone has to be adopted.

477. Therefore there is no (point in) the countering with defective objections, of the perception of him who sees the world of differences, since there is parity of welfare with the (scriptural) statement that apprehends the nature of Brahman, like "Brahman is knowledge, bliss."

L

478. There is no defect even in respect of the probans "being a body" because it is intended to mean "being the abode of enjoyment for those who have restrictions of each other." Nor is their failure of example; for there is possibility of the negative example in the case of the bodies of the yogins.

४७९. अत एव न व्यवस्थानिरुक्तिदौर्घट्यम्, सुखदुखाद्यनुसन्धानभावाभावरूपव्यवस्थाया अङ्गीकृतत्वात् ।

४८०. अतो भेदत्वहेतुरुपजीव्यविरोधान्न भेदमिथ्यात्वं साधयितुं प्रभवेदिति ।

४८१. किञ्च व्यवहारनिर्वाहकतया सत्यता च भेदस्य कुतो न स्यात् ?

४८२. ननु भेदस्य प्रत्यक्षादिविषयत्वेऽपि न तत्त्वावेदकप्रमाणविषयत्वम् । मैवम्; तत एव तत्साधनसम्भवात् ।

479. For the same reason there is no incongruity in the establishment of the regulation (of experience—vyavasthā); for there is the acceptance of the regulation (of experience) consisting in the existence and non-existence of the recollection of pleasure, pain etc.

480. Therefore because of the conflict with that which supports it (upajīvya), the probans "being difference" is not capable of establishing the illusory nature of difference.

481. Further why should not there be reality for difference as accounting for empirical usage?

482. Now, though difference is the content of a perception etc., still it is not the content of a means of valid knowledge that makes known the reality. Not so (says the siddhāntin); for even by that (former) it is possible to establish that (latter).

४८३. किञ्च धर्मित्वहेतुना तत्त्वावेदकप्रमाणवेद्यता च कुतो न भेदस्य स्यात्?

४८४. न चात्मनि धर्माभावः, आनन्दो विषयानुभवो नित्यत्वं चेति सन्ति धर्मा इत्यभ्युपगमात्। न परमार्थतो धर्मा इति चेन्न; नित्यत्वाद्यभावेऽनित्यत्वाद्यापातात्; तत्पक्षे पारमार्थिकस्यैव साधनाङ्गतानियमाभावाच्च।

४८५. चन्द्रभेदे धर्मित्वहेतोर्व्यभिचार इति चेत्—कोऽर्थः? चन्द्रभेदमात्राभाव इति वा, चन्द्राच्चन्द्रभेदाभाव इति वा।

483. Further why should not difference be the object of cognition by a means of valid knowledge making known the reality, because of the probans, "possessing an attribute"?

484. Nor is it that in the self there is no attribute; for it is admitted that there exist attributes *viz.*, bliss, experience of objects and eternality. If it be said that they are not attributes in absolute reality, no (says the siddhāntin), because of the contingence of non-eternality etc., in the non-existence of eternality etc., also because, according to that position, there is no restriction (to the effect) that only the absolutely real can serve as probans.

485. If it be said that there is inconstancy of the probans "possessing an attribute" in recpect of the difference in moons, what does this mean? Is it the non-existence of (all) difference as such from the moon (*i.e.*, difference from non-imposed moon as well as

४८६. आद्ये न व्यभिचारः, पक्षसमत्वात्। द्वितीये तस्यैवाभावेन धर्मित्वहेतोर्व्यभिचारस्य दूरतः परास्तत्वात्।

४८७. किञ्च भेदत्वहेतोरविद्यानिवृत्तिरूपमोक्षात्मभेदे व्यभिचारश्च। न च तयोर्भेद इति चेत्तर्ह्यात्मनोऽनादिनित्यतया तदभिन्नमोक्षस्य ज्ञानसाध्याविद्यानिवृत्तिरूपत्वानुपपत्तिः।

differences from the imposed moon), or the non-existence of the difference of (one) moon from the (other) moon (*i.e.*, no difference of real moon from a non-imposed moon)?

486. In the first case there is no inconstany (of the probans), since it is on a par with the subject. In the second case that (difference of moon from the non-imposed moon) being itself non-existent, the inconstancy (adduced in respect) of the probans "possessing an attribute" is refuted (even) at a distance; (hence there is no inconstancy).

LI

487. Besides, of the probans "being difference" there is also inconstancy in respect of the difference between release (mokṣa), which is of the form of removal of nescience, and the self. And if it be said that there is no difference between those two, then the self being beginninglessly eternal, it is not intelligible that release which is non-different from that (self) has the form of the removal of nescience, that has to be accomplished by knowledge.

४८८. अन्यतरचन्द्रस्यैवारोपितत्वेनारोपितानारोपितभेदे व्यभिचारश्च । मुक्तामुक्तभेदेऽनैकान्त्यं च ।

४८९. मुक्तामुक्तयोर्भेदोऽसिद्ध इति चेन्न; विमतो भिन्नो मुक्तत्वादिति तत्सिद्धेः । शुक्ताविव रजतमाविद्यको भेदो मुक्तेऽप्यङ्गीक्रियते इति चेन्न; मुक्तस्याविद्येति व्याहतेः ।

४९०. ननु किं भेदः परमात्मप्रतियोगिकः साध्यते? उत जीवप्रतियोगिकः? अथवा जडप्रतियोगिकः? आहोस्वित्सकलप्रतियोगिकः?

488. And there is the inconstancy (of the probans) in respect of the difference between the superimposed and the non-superimposed (moons) since only one of the two moons is superimposed. And there is the inconclusiveness (of the probans) in respect of the difference between the released (mukta) and the non-released (amukta).

LII

489. If it be said that there is non-establishment of difference between the released and the non-released, no (says the siddhāntin); for it is established thus: "those (selves) in dispute are different, because they are liberated." If It be said that just like the (illusory) silver in nacre, there is accepted (only) a nescience-created difference even of the liberated, no (says the siddhāntin); for there is the contradiction in (the words) "nescience of the liberated."

490. Now, is the difference established with the supreme self for its counter-correlate, or the (individual)

४९१. नाद्यः; परमात्मनि हेतोरनैकान्त्यात्; संसाराभावलक्षण-मुक्तत्वस्य तत्र सम्भवात्।

४९२. द्वितीयेऽपि सकलजीवप्रतियोगिकः स्वव्यतिरिक्तजीवप्रतियोगिको वा? नाद्यः; मुक्तस्यापि जीवत्वेनांशे बाधात्।

४९३. नोत्तरः; मुक्तस्य तद्भेदसिद्ध्या विना तेषामेतद्व्यतिरिक्तत्वासिद्ध्याप्रसिद्धविशेषणत्वात्; सिद्धौ च सिद्धसाधनत्वात्; सकलजीवप्रतियोगिकभेदसाधनस्य प्रकृतानुपयुक्तत्वेनार्थान्तरत्वाच्च।

self for its counter-correlate, or the inert (matter) for its counter-correlate, or everything for its counter-correlate?

491. Not the first, because the probans is inconculsive in respect of the supreme self, since there is the possibility there of the state of release consisting in the non-existence of the world (saṁsāra—cycle of births and deaths).

492. In the second too, has it all the (individual) selves for its counter-correlate or (all) selves other than itself for its counter-correlate? Not the first, because there is sublation in respect of part (of the subject) since the released (self) also is a self.

493. Not the latter, because since without the establishment of the difference of the released (self) from those (other selves), their being other than that (released self) is non-established, there is non-established probandum, and because if that (*i.e.*, being other) be established, there is (the defect of) the establishment of

४९४. अत एव न तृतीयः; नापि चतुर्थः; पूर्ववदंशे बाधाद्-प्रसिद्धविशेषणात्वाच्चेति ।

४९५. नैवम्——अविवक्षितप्रतियोगिविशेषस्य भेदस्य साध्यत्वात् ।

४९६. न चैवमर्थान्तरता, मुक्तस्य भेदमात्रमाक्षिपन्तं प्रति तत्साधनस्य संगतत्वात् ।

४९७. अथवा प्रागवस्थायां येन भेदेन विशिष्टः, तेनैव मोक्षेऽपीत्ययमर्थोऽत्राभिप्रेत इति न कश्चिद्दोष इति ।

the established; and (also) because the establishment of the difference which has all (individual) selves for its counter-correlate being useless for the present purpose, there is (the defect of the establishment of) the non-intended.

494. Hence too not the third. Nor the fourth; for as in the previous case, there are (the defects of) the sublation in respect of part (of the subject) and non-established probandum.

495. It is not so (says the siddhāntin); for the probandum is that difference for which no specified counter-correlate is intended.

496. And there is not thus (the defect of the establishment of) the unintended, because in regard to him who objects to difference as such for the released, it is appropriate to establish that (alone).

497. Or else, there is no defect since this is the meaning intended by us (Dvaitins) here, that in release too that (self) is qualified by that same

४९८. ननु किमिदं मुक्तत्वं नाम? किं संसारप्रध्वंसः, तत्संसर्गाभावो वा? नाद्यः; परमात्मन्यसिद्धेः; निगदादिदृष्टान्तस्य साधनवैकल्यापत्तेश्च। अत एव नोत्तर इति चेन्न; अविवक्षितविशेषसंसर्गाभावस्य हेतुत्वात्।

४९९. ननु चात्र सम्बन्धमात्राभावाधिकरणत्वं हेतुः। तत्राभावाधिकरणमात्रेणालम्, किं सम्बन्धमात्रग्रहणेन? अथवाधिकरणत्वमात्रं हेतुरस्तु, किमभावग्रहणेन? किञ्चाधिकरणं कारणविशेषः। तत्र किं विशेषग्रहणेन? एवं कारकं कारणविशेषः। तत्र किं विशेषग्रहणेनेति चेन्न।

difference, whereby it was qualified in the prior state (of saṁsāra).

498. "Now what is it that is meant by being released? Is it the posterior non-existence of worldly bondage (saṁsāra), or non-existence of relation thereto? Not the first, because it is not established in the supreme self (Paramātman), and because there is the contingence of the non-existence of the probans in the case of such examples as (these released from) chains etc. For the same reason it is not the latter". If this be said, no (says the siddhāntin); because the probans is that non-existence of relation whose specific nature is unintended.

499. "And now the probans here is 'being the substrate of non-existence of (all) relations as such'. That being so it is enough to (say) 'being the substrate of the mere non-existence (as such).' What is the use of taking (the words) 'all relations.' Or else, let the

५००. तथा सति प्रमेयत्वादीनामपि केवलान्वयित्वभङ्गात् । प्रमाविषयत्वं प्रमेयत्वम् । तत्र विषयत्वेनालम्, किं प्रमाग्रहणेनेत्यादेः तत्रापि सुवचत्वात् ।

५०१. यद्धेतुव्यवच्छेदकत्वेन पृथगुपादीयते तदेव विशेषणं प्रयोजनान्तरमपेक्षते ; न पुनस्तन्मात्रान्तरगतमिति चेत्समं प्रकृतेऽपि ।

५०२. अथवा संसारसंसर्गाभावो मुक्तत्वम् । तथात्वे घटो दृष्टान्तः ।

probans be merely 'being the substrate'; what is the use of taking (in the word) 'non-existence'? Besides, the substrate is one of the special causes. That being so what is the use of taking (in the word) 'special'? Similarly the causal-correlate is a special kind of cause; that being so what is the use of taking (in the word) 'special'?" If this be said, no.

500. For, in that case there would be the breakdown of the nature of merely positive concomitance even in the case of knowability etc. thus: knowability consists in being the content of knowledge; here "being the content" will do; what is the use of taking (in the word) "knowledge"? Such (objections) are easy to state there too.

501. "It is only such a qualification as is taken up for delimiting the probans, which stands in need of a distinct purpose, but not such as is contained in that (probans itself)". If this be said, there is parity (of this) in the present context too.

502. Or else, being released is the non-existence of relation to worldly bondage (samsara); in that case,

परमात्मप्रतियोगिको वा भेदोऽत्र साध्यः । बन्धप्रध्वंसाधिकरणत्वञ्च मुक्तत्वमिति न परमात्मनि व्यभिचारः ।

५०३. किञ्च मुक्तामुक्तयोर्भेदाभावे मुक्तस्य संसारः, संसारिणो वा मुक्तत्वं स्यात् ।

५०४. ननु मुक्तस्य संसारः स्यादिति किं संसाराधिकरणस्वरूपैणैक्यमापाद्यते? उत संसारानुभवः?

५०५. नाद्यः; इष्टापादनात् । अपाद्यापादकयोर्भेदाभावाच्च ।

pot is the example. Or the probandum here is the difference which has the supreme self (Paramātman) for its counter-correlate. And there is no inconstancy (of the probans) in respect of the supreme self, because to be released is to be the substrate of the posterior non-existence of worldly bondage (saṁsāra).

503. Besides, if there be no difference between the released and the non-released, then there would be worldly bondage for the released or releasedness for the one in worldly bondage.

504. Now (in the statement), "there would be worldly bondage for the released", is there deduced the identity of existence (svarūpa) with the substrate of worldly bondage, or the experience of worldly bondage?

505. Not the first, because it is deducing the desirable, and because there is non-difference between the (conclusion) deduced and the ground of deduction.

५०६. नोत्तरः ; अनुभवस्यान्तःकरणादिसापेक्षत्वात् , अंतःकरणादेश्चाज्ञानसापेक्षत्वात्, निवृत्ताविद्यस्य कार्यान्वयायोगात् ।

५०७. एवं संसारिणो मुक्तत्वं स्यादिति कोऽर्थः ? किं संसाराधिकरणस्वरूपस्यैव मुक्तत्वं स्यादिति ? किं वा संसारिण एव सतो मुक्तत्वानुभवः स्यादिति ?

५०८. नाद्यः ; पूर्ववदिष्टापादनात् । नोत्तरः ; संसारिणो मुक्ताद्भेदसद्भावात् ।

५०९. मुक्तस्य संसारिणो भेदाभावे कथं संसारिणो मुक्ताद्भेद इति

506. Not the latter, because experience is dependent on the internal organ etc., because internal organ etc., are dependent on nescience, and for him whose nescience has disappeared, the persistence of the product (of nescience) is impossible.

507. Likewise, what is the meaning of (the statement) "there would be releasedness for the one in worldly bondage"? Is it that there would be releasedness for the very one whose existence (svarūpa) was the substrate of worldly bondage or that even while being one in worldly bondage there would be the experience of releasedness?

508. Not the first since, as in the prior case, it is deducing the desirable. Not the latter because there is difference for the one in worldly bondage from the released.

509. If it be asked how, when for the released there is no difference from the one in worldly bondage,

चेत्—भवेदेवं यद्ययं भेदो वास्तवः स्यात् । अज्ञानकृतो हि मुक्तात्संसारिणो भेदः । सोऽज्ञानिनः संसारिणः प्रतीयते, न निवृत्ताज्ञानस्य मुक्तस्येति कात्रानुपपत्तिरिति चेन्न ।

५१०. यद्यज्ञानकृतो भेदः तर्हीश्वस्याज्ञानाभावात्संसारिणैक्यं तेनानुभूयेत । अनुभूयते इति चेत्, यदीश्वरः संसारिणैक्यमनुभवेत्तर्हि दुःखी स्यात् । न चैवम् । ततो नेश्वरस्य संसारिणैक्यानुभवो ऽङ्गीकर्तुमुचितः ।

५११. यदुक्तं मुक्तस्यान्तःकरणाद्यभावान्न संसारानुभवप्राप्तिरिति,

there is difference for the one in worldly bondage from the released, (the Advaitin answers that) it would be so, if the difference (that is deduced) were real. The difference for the one in worldly bondage from the released is indeed a product of nescience. That is cognised for the nescience-tainted one in worldly bondage, not for the released from whom nescience has disappeared. Thus, what is it that is unintelligible here? If this be said, no (says the Dvaitin):

510. If difference were the effect of nescience then since there is no nescience in the Lord, there should be experienced by Him identity with the one in worldly bondage. If it be said that it is experienced, (then) in case the Lord experiences identity with the one in worldly bondage, he would be the experiencer of sorrow; and it is not thus. So it is not proper to accept the Lord's experience of identity with the one in worldly bondage.

511. And for the statement that there is not the contingence of experience of worldly bondage for the

तदसत्; निर्विशेषत्वादेकरसे चैतन्येऽन्तःकरणसंसर्गभावाभावयोरप्ययोगात्।

५१२. अज्ञानसद्भावाभावाभ्यां सम्भवत इति चेन्न। तदपि तादृगेव।

५१३. किञ्चेश्वरवचनैस्तस्य संसारिभेदानुभव एवानुमीयते। कुतस्तत्राभेदानुभवप्रत्याशा।

तान्यहं वेद सर्वाणि न त्वं वेत्थ परन्तप।
सुखं दुःखं भवोऽभावो भयञ्चाभयमेव च।

इत्यादिभिः।

released because of the non-existence of the internal organ etc. (for him), that is not sound. For in the case of the intelligence which, because of being attributeless, is homogeneous in essence, even the existence and non-existence of relation to the internal organ are not possible.

512. If it be said that they are possible because of the existence and non-existence of nescience, no; (for) that too is only like that (unsuitable).

513. Further, from the (following) words of the Lord, there is inferred only His experiences of difference from the one in worldly bondage. Why then the obstinate desire for establishing the experience of identity for Him?

"I (Kṛṣṇa) know them all; you (Arjuna), O terror of the enemies, do not know (them)."
"Pleasure, pain, creation, existence, fear, fearlessness (of creatures proceed from Me)."

From these and other (statements, there is the inference).

५१४. किञ्च विमतो भेदो मुक्तौ न निवर्तते, ईश्वरेणानुभूयमानत्वात्, स्वरूपवदिति तत्सिद्धिः।

५१५. नन्वीश्वरेणानुभूयमानोऽपि मुक्तौ निवर्तताम्? किं विपक्षे बाधकमिति चेन्न।

५१६. यदीश्वरेणानुभूयमानोऽपि बाध्यते तर्हीश्वरस्य भ्रान्तत्वं प्रसज्येत, बाध्यशुक्तिकारजतद्रष्टृवत्। तस्य त्वभ्रान्तत्वात्तेनानुभूयमानो ब्रह्मात्मभेदो निवर्तते इति सिद्धम्।

५१७. अपर आह—नेश्वरेण स्वस्मात्संसारिणो भेददर्शनेऽपि

514. Further, by this (inference) "the difference under dispute does not disappear with release, because it is experienced by the Lord, like his own form (svarūpa)" that (difference) is established.

515. "Now though it be experienced by the Lord, let it disappear in release. What is the sublater in (maintaining the) opposite view?" If this be asked, no.

516. If there be sublation even for what is experienced by the Lord, then there is the contingence of the deludedness of the Lord, as for him who cognises the sublatable shell-silver. Since, however, He is not deluded, the difference between Brahman and the self experienced by him does not disappear: this is established.

517. Another one says, "though by the Lord is cognised the difference of the one in worldly bondage

मुक्तस्य भेदः सिद्धयति । न हि वयं मायावादिन इव जीवब्रह्मणोर्जीवानां वा भेदमपारमार्थिकं ब्रूमः, किन्तूपाधिकृतमेव ।

५१८. अतः पारमार्थिकत्वादीश्वरेणानुभूयमानत्वं युज्यते । औपाधिकत्वादुपाधिनाशे मुक्तौ तन्नाशात्स्वाभाविकाभेदः सिद्धयतीति ।

५१९. तदसत्, अभेदस्य स्वाभाविकत्वे सुखदुःखाद्यनुसन्धानप्रसङ्गात् । न हि चैतन्यैक्यं स्वाभाविके वर्तमाने सुखदुःखाद्यननुसन्धानं क्वचिद्दृष्टम् ।

५२०. ननु वयं जीवान्ब्रह्मणोऽशानभ्युपगच्छामः । तत्र किमंशा-

from Himself, still the difference for the released is not established. For we do not, like those who uphold the doctrine of Māya (Māyāvādins), say that the difference between the self and Brahman or among the selves is non-real, but (that) it is the product of adjuncts.

518. Hence because of being real, it stands to reason that it is experienced by the Lord. Because of being due to adjuncts, it (*i.e.* difference) is destroyed when the adjunct is destroyed at release; hence there is establishment for natural non-difference.

519. That is not sound (says the siddhāntin); for if non-difference be natural, then there is the contingence of the recollection of (one another's) pleasure, pain, etc. There is not indeed cognised anywhere the non-recollection of pleasure, pain, etc., when there exists natural identity of intelligence.

520. "Now, we admit the individual selves as parts of Brahman. Here, is there deduced reciprocal

नामन्योन्यानुसन्धानमापाद्यते, उतांशिनः। नाद्यः; हस्तपादाद्यवच्छिन्नात्मांशानां तदभावात्; औपाधिकभेदस्य सत्वात्। अत एव नोत्तर इति चेन्न।

५२१. अंशिनः परमेश्वरस्यैव स्वाभाविकाभेदे सकलजनसुखदुःखाद्यनुसन्धानापादनात्।

५२२. ननूक्तमत्र जीवेश्वरयोः स्वभावेनाभेदेऽप्युपाधिकृतभेदस्य सत्वान्न जीवगतसुखदुःखादिप्राप्तिरीश्वरस्येति।

५२३. तन्न; हस्तपादाद्युपाधिभेदेऽपि भोक्तुरेकत्वानुभवात्।

recollection as among the parts or that which has parts (*i.e.* the whole)? Not the first because that (recollection) does not exist for the parts of the self delimited by hands, feet, etc., since difference due to adjuncts is real. For the same reason not the latter (alternative)." If this be said, no (says the siddhāntin).

521. For if it is in the case of the Supreme Lord Himself, who has the parts (*i.e.* who is the whole) that there is natural non-difference, there is deduced recollection of the pleasure the pain etc., of all persons.

522. Now it has been said with regard to this, that even if there is natural non-difference between individual self and the Lord, yet since there is the difference produced by adjunct there do not result for the Lord the pleasures, pain, etc., present in the individual self.

523. That is not (sound); for in spite of differences due to adjuncts like hands, feet, etc., there is admitted the oneness of the enjoyer.

५२४. ननु संश्लिष्टोपाधित्वमनुसंधाने प्रयोजकम् । तदभावात्प्रकृते नानुसन्धानमिति चेत्—किमुपाधिसंश्लेषमात्रं प्रयोजकमुत स्वरूपैक्ये सति ?

५२५. नाद्यः; मातृसुखादेर्गर्भस्थेनानुसन्धानप्रसङ्गात् । नोत्तरः; स्वरूपैक्यमात्रस्य प्रयोजकत्वे सम्भवति विशेषणप्रक्षेपे प्रमाणाभावात् । तस्मात्स्वरूपाभेदेऽनुसन्धानमपरिहार्यम् ।

५२६. तदेवं जीवेश्वरभेदस्यौपाधिकत्वे स्वाभाविकाभेदेनेश्वरस्य जीवगतसुखदुःखाद्यनुसन्धानप्रसङ्गस्यावर्जनीयत्वात्, तदङ्गीकारस्य च प्रमाण-विरुद्धत्वात्, स्वाभाविक एव जीवेश्वरभेदः, न त्वौपाधिकः ।

524. " Now the determinant of recollection is the conjoined nature of the adjuncts ; because of its absence there is no recollection in the present context." If this be said, is the mere conjoining of adjuncts the determinant or (only) when there is identity of the entity (svarūpa) too ?

525. Not the first, because of the contingence of the recollection of the Mother's pleasure etc., by the child in the womb. Not the latter ; for when it is possible for the identity of the entity alone to be the determinant, there is no authority for introducing a qualification. Therefore where there is non-difference of entity, recollection cannot be avoided.

526. Thus, therefore, since, if the difference between the individual self and the Lord be due to adjunct, the contingence of the Lord's recollection, due to natural non-difference, of the pleasure, pain, etc., present in the individual self, cannot be avoided, and since its

५२७. किञ्च विमतो भेदः पारमार्थिकः, असद्व्यतिरिक्तत्वात्, ब्रह्म-वदित्यनुमानबाधितत्वाच्च न भेदत्वसाधनं भेदमिथ्यात्वे मानमिति सिद्धम् ।

५२८. अत एव विमतानि शरीराणि देवदत्तस्यैव भोगायतनानि; शरीरत्वात्, संप्रतिपन्नवत्—इत्याद्यनुमानं प्रत्यक्षबाधितम्, परस्परसुखदुः-खाद्यनुसंधानप्रसंगपराहतं च इति ।

५२९. विमतानि कलत्राणि देवदत्तस्यैव भोगायतनानि; कलत्र-त्वात्, सम्प्रतिपन्नवत्—इत्याद्यनुमानाभाससमानयोगक्षेमतयापहास्यम् ।

acceptance is opposed to (all) authority, the difference between the individual self and the Lord is natural, and not due to adjuncts.

527. And further because of being sublated by the inference "the difference under dispute is real, because it is different from the unreal, like Brahman" it is established that the probans "being different" is not the authority for (the establishment of) the illusory nature of difference.

LIII

528. For the same reason, any inference like the following: "the bodies under dispute are objects of enjoyment for Devadatta alone, because of being bodies, like the admitted (body)" is sublated by perception, and is refuted by the contingence of the reciprocal recollection of pleasure, pain, etc.

529. It is to be ridiculed because of parity of welfare with a fallacious inference, "the wives under

५३०. जयतीर्थमुनीन्द्रेण बालबोधाय निर्मितम् ।
वाङ्मुखाद्वाङ्मुखं भूयात्प्रीत्यै माधवमध्वयोः ॥

इति वादावली समाप्ता ।

dispute are the objects of enjoyment for Devadatta alone, because of being wives, like the admitted (wife)."

530. This discourse compiled by the venerable sage Jayatīrtha for the instructions of the learners, out of the discourses (of S'rī Madhva) may it be for the pleasure of Madhava (Viṣṇu) and Madhva.

THUS ENDS THE VĀDĀVALĪ

NOTES

[The Roman figures denote the main divisions indicated in the translation and the figures within brackets denote the sections].

I (1). Jayatīrtha the great Dvaita Vedāntin offers his prayers to Lord Viṣṇu and asks for his grace. It is the traditional practice with the writers on Vedānta to set out briefly the thesis of the work they propose to write in the opening verse of the work. The *Vādāvalī* proposes to establish the absolute reality of the universe as against the Advaitins' contention that it is illusory. The commentator Rāghavendra points out that the meditation of Brahman advocated by the author of the *Vedānta-sūtra*, Bādarāyaṇa, has for its object the perfect Brahman (Madhva points out that the term Brahman means the abode of infinite auspicious attributes). The reason for the assertion of the perfection of Brahman is stated in the second sūtra *i.e.*, because He is the creator, sustainer, etc., of this universe. If the created universe proves to be unreal, its creator's perfection would also become unreal; once His perfection becomes unreal meditation of him is meaningless. In order to establish the necessity and propriety of the meditation of Brahman advocated in the *Vedānta sūtras*, Jayatirtha proposes to establish the absolute reality of the universe through an elaborate criticism and refutation of the Advaitins' argument establishing the illusory nature of the universe.

The first line in the invocatory verse is the substance of the first *sūtra* and the second line, of the second *sūtra*. When God is said to be the creator of the universe, He is the efficient cause and not the material cause. It must be noted that the *Sattā* of the soul is not created by God, but is dependent on Him. He is not the *Sattā-prada*, but the *sattā* is in His *ādhīna i.e.*, (it is dependent on Him). Eight-fold functions are attributed to God (1) *utpattī*=creation, (2) *Sthiti*= maintenance, (3) *Saṁhāra*-destruction, (4) *Niyamana*=control, (5) *Jñāna*=knowledge, (6) *ajñāna*=nescience, (7) *Bandha* Bondage and (8) *Mokṣā*=liberation.

II (2). Jayatīrtha's reference to Viṣṇu as the creator, sustainer, etc., of the real universe is objected to by the *pūrvapakṣin* on the ground that the universe is not real. As the illusory nature of the universe is clearly established by scripture and other pramāṇas, the Advaita writer Ānandabodha in his *Nyāyamakaranda* sets forth the three inferences to establish the illusory nature of the universe. The Advaitin's inference proceeds with three probans, namely cognisablity, inertness and finitude. The subject of the inference is " that in reference to which there is dispute—whether it is illusory or absolutely real." That is to say it is other than Brahman, the uncreated and the barely phenomenal. The subject should have been stated as follows; the world under dispute, that is other than Brahman, non-existence and apparent reality. The statement of the subject by the use of only one word is attributable to the principle of parsimony.

III (3). Mithyātva *i.e.*, the probandum in the above inference is undefined. The probandum in any inference must be known as existing somewhere, in some place other than the subject (Pakṣa). No Knowledge of the probandum is possible where it is indefinable. Inference can be of no help to us where we do not have the knowledge of the probandum.

In Advaita literature mithyātva is defined in the seven forms mentioned. Jayatīrtha proposes to examine each of the definitions in detail. In the criticism of the Advaitin's inference Jayatīrtha first directs his attack against the defects of the probandum. For a statement of alternatives 3—7 see *Tattvapradīpikā* (2nd edition), p. 33; for the Advaitin's refutátion of the Dvaita criticism, see

Advaitasiddhi (Advaitamañjari), p. 9 'establishing alternatives (3) and (7).

IV (4-15). Jayatirtha points out in the rest of the text that not one of the alternative explanations of illusoriness holds water. Of this it cannot be the first. The second alternative is further resolved into two alternatives *i.e.*, the content that is lacking it, real or unreal. Both the alternatives are rejected on the ground of the defect of overpervasion in respect of *Asat* and *Brahman.* According to the Advaitin neither is illusory. The probans "being different from sat" is found in asat, which is not illusory. The probans "being different from asat" is found in Brahman that is not illusory. Hence the defect of overpervasion.

The difference predicated with reference to indeterminability has for its counter-correlate the real-and-the-unreal together. The Dvaitin no doubt admits that the universe is non-different from real. This does not prevent him from pointing out that the universe is different from the real-and-the-unreal together. The Dvaitin secures the difference from the real for the universe by taking the instance of Brahman, because that is what the Advaitin understands by real. We must not fail to note the fact that Madhva admits difference between reals. In fact according to him there are no two perfectly identical things. This fact is brought out by his doctrine of fivefold differences (pañcabheda).

The interpretation of the term indeterminability as "not being the locus of reality and unreality" fares no better at the hands of the Dvaitin. The Dvaitin admits that the universe is not at the same time the locus of the real and the unreal. The adduced defect, namely, establishment of the established is still there.

The quotation "that which is not indeterminable" is from Citsukha's *Tattvapradīpikā* (p. 79). The main objection of the Dvaitin is not that the probandum indeterminability is not cognised anywhere. We should note the fact that the Dvaitin's analysis of reality admits of no compromise. There is no half way house between the real and the unreal. The law of the excluded middle applies to reality and admits of no exception. Whatever is not real is unreal; whatever is not unreal is real. The disjunction is complete. They don't admit a non-descript *tertitum quid*.

The Advaitin maintains that the two-fold differences predicated by him with reference to indeterminability are not to be taken as absolutely real. There would result contradiction only when we have two really opposed negations in one and the same locus. Where the negations are not absolutely real, there is no scope for contradiction. (See *Tattvapradīpikā*, p. 16).

The Advaitin is of opinion that the universe cannot be determined in terms of the real and the unreal. So he calls it, "different from the real and the unreal." But he maintaines that it is the indeterminable nature of the universe in terms of the real and the unreal that has led him to describe them as different from either. The differences should not be taken as real. The word *only* is significant for the Advaitin who wants only to establish that the universe cannot be defined in terms of the real and the unreal. He does not affirm the difference from the real or the unreal predicated about the Universe.

The Dvaitin urges as against this argument, "because the universe cannot be determined in terms of inderminability let him describe it as the opposite of indeterminability." The Dvaitin has stated two pervasions: (1) wherever there is the non-existence of unreality, there is reality; (2) wherever there is non-existence of reality, there is unreality. The Advaitin urges that these pervasions are not established, and as long as they are not established the Dvaitin cannot treat the Advaitin's description of the universe as contradictory. The Dvaitin holds that the prevasion can be secured in the Ātman *i.e.*, the Brahman. In the Brahman there is the absence of unreality, and the presence of reality.

V (16-25). The Advaitin points out that the pervasion between reality and the non-existence of unreality put forth by the Dvaitin in the case of Ātman is conditioned by the adjunct ātmatva. The Dvaitin in reply analysis the term *ātmatva* into eight alternatives and refutes them one after another.

The Nyāya definition of generality is that it is eternal, one, and abides in many. As Ātmatva is present only in Brahman and not anywhere else, it is impossible to treat it as a generality. The Advaitin in reply contends that there is possibility for generality on the ground of the presence of the assumptive differences in the ātman. The Dvaitin's answer to this objection is that such assumptively different ātmans form a part of the subject, because all that is illusory is treated as the subject. Hence ātmatva cannot be an upādhi and no counter-argument in the form "the world is not real, because it is anātma" would be tenable because of partial non-establishment of the *probans* "ātmatva".

The *second* alternative, reality (sattvam), happens to be the probandum itself. Hence there is the defect of non-difference of the probans and the probandum. The *third* alternative, unsublatability, is found in non-existence and there is no probandum there. Hence the inconstancy of the pervasion. The *fourth* alternative, knowledgeness, is found in the subject, because vṛtti-jñāna is also a kind of knowledge; hence ātmatva cannot be an upādhi. The *fifth* alternative, being the substrate of knowledge, is not found in the ātman though it is real. Hence the inconstancy of the pervasion. Ātman according to Advaita is not a knowing entity. There is no substrate-attribute relation in it. The *sixth* alternative, self-luminosity, is discussed when the criticism of the probans, *i.e.*, cognisability is taken up (XV ff). The *seventh* and the *eighth* alternatives are not found in the ātman. The advaitin's Brahman admits of no predication, for the reason that there is nothing outside it.

The Advaitin finds fault with the Dvaitin for the analysis of the term ātmatva, on the ground that such an entity is established for the Dvaitin. The resourceful Dvaitin turns round and retorts that whatever alternatives may be acceptable to the Dvaitin, they are all defect-ridden for the Advaitin. The Dvaitin concludes that the Advaitin's position that the universe is different from the real and the unreal is contradictory.

VI (26-42). The siddhāntin refutes the inference urged to establish indeterminability. The commentator states the inference in full: "what is under dispute is different from the real and the unreal, because it is sublatable, like Brahman as a negative instance". Some logicians are of opinion that the non-established qualification is no defect at all, and others are of opinion that it is a defect. The school that holds the opinion that it is a defect argues that a non-established qualification obstructs our cognition of pervasion. Thus it taints the inference. As against this, certain neo-logicians point out that the definition of the subject (pakṣa) should not include the term "doubt". In negative pervasion where the probandum is a negation there is no need for the establishment of the qualification; so it is urged that the non-established qualification is no defect at all.

The defect is alleged from the opponent's point of view. S'rī Madhva is of opinion that "ās'rayāsiddhi", "vyadhikaraṇāsiddhi," etc., are not defects. They are cases of the defects of the positive instances.

In this inference of the Advaitin there is not the defect of non-established qualification. The subject in the inference is reality and unreality. If any one of them by itself is taken as the subject there is the non-fulfilment of the object for which the inference is used. The purpose of the inference is to establish that the universe is different from the real and the unreal. Such a position cannot be established with reality or unreality alone as the subject. Further there will be the defect of the establishment of the established if only one term (the real or the unreal) is treated as the subject. So the subject comprises two terms reality and unreality. The probandum is "being the counter-correlate of absolute non-existence located in a single entity." The statement of the probandum in this manner helps the Advaitin to get over the defect of the non-established probandum. The positive instance cited is colour and taste. In this positive instance there is the probandum "being the counter-correlate of the absolute non-existence located in a single entity". Let us assume Vāyu (air) as the single entity. In Vāyu there is the absolute non-existence both of colour and taste. There is the probans 'being an attribute."

The Davaitin criticises the inference in detail. The term "vastu" in the inference means reality, and as such that part of the subject cannot be the counter-correlate of the non-existence present in itself. Hence the contradiction. The probans is inconstant in respect of knowability and nameability. These two attributes are not absent from any place. They are called kevalānvayi dharmas. As such there is no non-existence for them. Hence the probandum "being the counter-correlate of absolute non-existence located in a single entity" is not found in them. The probans, "being an attribute" is present there. Hence the inconstancy. Besides this, the inference is conditioned by an adjunct "being non-contradictory". An adjunct is that which is pervasive with the probandum and non-pervasive with the probans. "Being non-contradictory" is found in all those places where the probandum is present. Let us take the example itself, *i.e.* colour and taste. There is the adjunct there. Colour and taste are not opposed. They are found together in the fruit. The adjunct is not pervasive of the probans. The probans "being an attribute" is present in the subject. The adjunct is not there for the simple reason that reality and unreality are contradictories.

An unacceptable counter-inference like the one formulated by the Advaitin is put forth by the Dvaitin. There is only a slight modification in the counter-inference. The term "vastu" is replaced by the term Dharmi (substrate). The conclusion reached by the counter-inference is not acceptable to the Advaitin, because there is no one substrate in which there is the non existence of the potness as well as the non-existence of non-potness.

The Advaitin makes use of "presumption" (a pramāṇa) to prove indeterminability. He states two general rules pertaining to reality and unreality. The real cannot be sublated, and the unreal cannot be cognised. (See *Tattvapradīpikā*, p. 76). The universe is sublated as well as cognised. Sublatability and cognisability cannot be accounted for except by the presumption that the universe is neither real nor unreal. This Pramāṇa according to Madhva is subsumed under inference. The presumption in this case can be expressed in the form of an inference: "what is under dispute is indeterminable, because it is sublatable as well as cognisable."

The Dvaitin with a view to point out the inconstancy of the pervasion in the presumptive argument proposes first to examine the term "sat" in the counter-argument urged with a view to establish the presumptive arguments. If it is interpreted as one that possesses reality, then the universe which possesses reality is sublatable, according to Advaita; and as such there is the contradiction of the following pervasion of the Advaitin "that which is real is not sublatable". It may be contended that there is no sublation of the universe in empirical state. The Dvaitin replies that in vyavahāra stage inference does establish the sublatable nature of the universe. There are certain errors like the perceptions of the blue colour in the Ākāśa which are not at all sublated. There would be non-difference with them for reality. If it is interpreted as that which is unsublatable there would result the defect of the non-difference of the subject from the probandum. It cannot be the third for the reason that the Dvaitins accept that Brahman is unsublatable. Hence the defect of the establishment of the established.

The Dvaitin analysis the statement that "the unreal is not cognised". What is it, that is not cognised? Is it the cognition of the unreal as unreal? If that is so, then there would be no empirical usage in respect of the unreal. If the cognition of the unreal as real be denied, there would be no empirical usage in respect of delusion, because the very definition of delusion is the apprehension of the unreal as real. If it be contended that what is deluded is indeterminable, then is that indeterminable cognised as indeterminable, or, as otherwise? If it be cognised as it is, then there could be no empirical usage about delusion, because the indeterminable is cognised as indeterminable. If it be cognised as otherwise, then there is the violation of the statement that the unreal is not cognised. On this ground there is no possibility of erroneous cognition. (For Advaitins refutation of the criticism, see *Advaita siddhi*, p. 121).

VII (43). The second alternative referred to (the second of the first seven alternatives stated in the beginning of the text, *i.e.* unreality). The Dvaitin points out that it cannot be unreality. Indeterminability according to the Advaitin is other than both the real and the unreal. The statement that indeterminability is unreality is opposed to Advaita.

VIII (44-60). The Dvaitin examines the third alternative "being different from the real". He resolves this again into four alternatives. Is it parā jāti (summum genus), or being not Brahman, or unreality, or being other than unsublatability. In the first case there is the defect of apasiddhānta (being opposed to the doctrines of one's own school). The advaitin does not deny the presence of generality in the universe. In the second case, *i.e.* "being not Brahman", there is the defect of the establishment of the established, because the Dvaitins admit that the universe is not Brahman. In the third case *i.e.* unreality, there is opposition to their own school of thought, because the Advaitins do not admit that the universe is unreal. They hold that it is indeterminable *i.e.* being other than the real and the unreal. In the fourth case there is the defect of the establishment of the established. The Dvaitin admits that the universe is other than the unsublatable. The unsublatable is Brahman, and the universe is other than Him. Hence the defect of the establishment of the established. If the term "being other than the unsublatable" is interpreted as *sublatability*, the Dvaitin proceeds to resolve the sense of the term into two. (*a*) Is sublatability an erroneously cognised object or (*b*) is it being the counter-correlate of negation in the locus of the cognition? It cannot be the first. The Dvaitins too have admitted that kind of sublatability for the universe. The universe which is delusively cognised as indeterminable is validly cognised by the Dvaitin as real. Hence the defect of the establishment of the established. The second alternative is resolved into two; the negation in reference to the locus, is it at a particular place and time, or is it in all three times, and all places? In the first case there is the defect of the establishment of the established in respect of a part of the subject. In the second case there is contradiction in relation to a part of the subject. Eternal and omnipresent Akās'a and Time form a part of the subject. They can never become the counter-correlates of the non-existence in respect of all three times and all places. Hence the contradiction.

The commentator discusses in this connection whether Ākās'a and Time are eternal and omnipresent. There are scriptural declarations to the effect that Ākās'a emerged out of Ātman, and night and day are created. The scripture in these contexts refers to the elemental Ākās'a and secondary Time. The Ākās'a and Time referred to by the Dvaitin are not primary ones. It is called Avyākṛta Ākās'a and not Bhūtākās'a. The Time referred to is Mahākāla. They are eternal and omnipresent. They are cognised by witness-conciousness.

The Dvaitin examines the term "being cognised" and resolves it into the two following alternatives. Is it being validly cognised, or delusively cognised? The first alternative leads to the defect of undue extension.

The Dvaitin points out that the term negation (niṣedha) can mean two things:—It may mean cognition of non-existence, or cognition of "being different from the real." It cannot be the first because of the contingence of absolute unreality. It cannot be the second for the reason that the Advaitin has not yet explained the term "being different from the real".

IX (61-68). The Dvaitin examines the fourth alternative "not being a content of Pramāṇa". He resolves the sense of the term into two: (1) not being a content of some one pramāṇa or (2) not being a content of any pramāṇa at all. It cannot be the first, because the Dvaitin admits that attributes like odour are not contents of some pramāṇa like the sense of hearing. Hence the defect of the establishment of the established. It cannot be the second, because of the contingency in respect of Brahman becoming illusory. Brahman according to Advaita is not the object of any pramāṇa.

Besides, it is impossible to define the universe as the subject because it is said to be not the content of any pramāṇa. In the absence of pramāṇas we cannot have any knowledge. Hence the difficulty of defining the universe as the subject. If it be contended that the universe is known through perception which cognises the phenomenal and as such it is impossible to define the universe as the subject, no says the siddhāntin. There is no pramāṇa to the effect that perception cognises only the phenomenal contents. It may be that because of the unreality of the objects that perception cognises, it is said to cognise phenomenal objects.

The Dvaitin asks, "how do we know that the objects of perception are only phenomenal?" The statement that something is a pramāṇa and yet cognises only the phenomenal contents is contradictory. The term pramāṇa means valid cognition. It is contradictory to state that valid cognition cognises phenomenal objects. If that which cognises phenomenal objects is pramāṇa there is nothing to prevent us from regarding the shell-silver cognition as pramāṇa. The Dvaitin constructs an inference and draws a conclusion opposed to Advaita: "pramāṇa cognises the non-phenomenal, because it is a pramāṇa, like the non-dual texts." One is tāttvika pramāṇa and the other is atāttvika pramāṇa. The argument is based on the Advaitin's theory of threefold reality. The Dvaitin points out that such an argument is valid only after the establishment of the threefold nature of reality and not prior to it.

X (69-70). The Dvaitin examines the fifth alternative *i.e.*, being the content of an invalid cognition. It is acceptable to the Dvaitin. Hence the defect of the establishment of the established. S'rī Madhva is of opinion that everything in the universe is real. His test for reality is that it must have existed at some time. For a thing to be real it need not be eternal. So he regards the Advaitin's statement that " the universe is indeterminable " and the Buddhists statement that " the universe is momentary " and the atheistic Sāṅkhyan's statement that " the universe is a modification of Prakṛti " as invalid. The Dvaitin is opposed to all the three doctrines, Vivartavāda, Kṣaṇikavāda, and Pariṇāmavāda. God, according to Dvaita Vedānta is the nimitta-kāraṇa (efficient cause) of the universe. He does not create the universe out of nothing; He is just like the potter, with this difference that He is omnicient.

XI (71-88). The Dvaitin examines the sixth alternative *i.e.*, " nescience." Is nescience the beginningless indeterminable, or the beginningless positive existent that is destroyed by the cognition, or the material cause of the delusion ? All these three modes of definition are vatiated by defects. It cannot be the beginningless indeterminable, because indeterminability as such is not yet established. The non-establishment of indeterminability leads to the defect of the non-established qualification. Besides, the definition as what is beginningless and indeterminable is overpervasive in respect of Ākās'a. Ākās'a is beginningless as well as indeterminable. The adduced overpervasion is refuted on the ground that Ākās'a is not beginningless, because of the non-existence of beginninglessness in any entity other than Brahman. The Dvaitin points out that in that case nescience too cannot be beginningless; hence the definition is inapplicable.

The second definition is taken up for criticism *i.e.*, " a beginningless positive entity, destroyable by cognition ". This definition is inapplicable because in nescience there is the absence of the attribute " beginninglessness ". For the Advaitin no entity other than Brahman is beginningless in the plenary sense of the term

Hence its absence from nescience. Further it is unintelligible for us to admit destruction by cognition for what is beginningless and existent. Brahman is beginningless and positive and it is not destroyed by any cognition. The same position holds good in the case of nescience also.

To this the Advaitin replies that the term "positive entity" is used with reference to nescience in a figurative sense. It does not in reality mean a positive entity. The term signifies that it is different from non-existence. The siddhāntin replies that the intended significance of the term "positive entity" alone will do for the purpose of establishing the non-destruction by cognition for the beginningless existent, on the analogy of Brahman. Instead of a positive existent we have in its place the beginningless being different from non-existence; the same analogy holds good in the case of nescience also.

The Advaitin contents that the Dvaitin's inference is conditioned by the adjunct "self-hood." The Dvaitin's inference is as follows. "That which is a beginningless and positive entity is destroyed by cognition, because it is a beginningless and positive entity like Brahman." The adjunct self-hood is present wherever there is the probandum. If Brahman is the probandum, self-hood also is there. Thus the pervasion between the adjunct and probandum is secured. The adjunct must be non-pervasive in respect of the probans, *i.e.*, "beginningless and positive entity". This is present in the subject and there is no self-hood there. Thus the non-pervasion in respect of the probans is secured for the adjunct.

The Dvaitin points out the inconstancy of the pervasion of the probandum by the adjunct in respect of absolute non-existence. Absolute non-existence is not destroyed by cognition. Being not destroyed by cognition is the probandum. It is present in absolute non-existence and the adjunct selfhood is not there. Hence the inconstancy of the pervasion. Thus it is established that the adduced adjunct is defective. Therefore the inference is not conditioned by an adjunct.

The Dvaitin examines the third alternative, namely "being the material cause of delusion". What is it that is meant by the term "delusion"? Is it the content of the delusive cognition, or the delusive cognition itself? It cannot be the content of the delusive cognition, because it is unreal; and for the unreal there is no material cause. It cannot be the second, because the definition "being the material cause of delusive cognition" is overpervasive in respect of the internal organ. The internal organ is the material cause of the cognition in general. Further the definition is also inapplicable, because nescience is not directly the material cause of the delusive cognition.

The Advaitin points out that non-acceptance of the position that nescience is the material cause of delusion would result in the admission of the reality for the delusive cognition. The Dvaitin points that such a position is acceptable to him. The Advaitin points out that the acceptance of the reality of the delusive cognition contradicts the possibility of sublation. If the delusive cognition is to be real, there should be no sublating cognition as invalid knowledge; but there is the sublating cognition. So the delusive cognition is not real. The sublating cognition denies the reality of the content of the cognition. The Advaitin's argument leads to the conclusion that if the content of the cognition is real, the cognition is real.

XII (89-130). The Dvaitin after dismissing the definition of nescience, proceeds to point out that nescience has no pramāṇa. It is not nescience as such that has no pramāṇa; but it is nescience as defined by the Advaitin that has no pramāṇa. The Dvaitin also admits a kind of nescience that is beginningless; but it is not indeterminable.

The Advaitin puts forth this inference to establish the positive nature of nescience. (See *Tattvapradīpikā*, p. 58). The subject of the inference is Devadatta's valid cognition and the probandum is positive nescience. It has to be established; so it cannot be stated barely. If it is barely stated, the Dvaitin would urge the defect of non-established qualification; so it is stated in an indirect manner. The valid cognition of Devadatta *i.e.*, the subject, destroys its anterior non-existence as well as the positive nescience. To secure the intended meaning we have to exclude anterior non-existence: so the following words "being other than anterior non-existence" are used. The probans is "being valid knowledge". This is in the subject *i.e.*, Devadatta's valid cognition. The example is the undisputed valid cognition. Let us take one Rama's valid cognition; there is the probans, "being a valid cognition". There is the presence of the probandum also there. Rāma's valid cognition destroys what is beginningless and other than the anterior non-existence of Devadatta's valid cognition.

The Dvaitin criticises the Advaitin's inference by erecting a counter-inference yielding conclusions that are not acceptable and desirable to the Advaitin. The commentator states the inference in detail; "Caitra's desire has for its material cause something other than that which produces it and is unsublatable, because it is a desire, like Maitra's." This inference is unacceptable to Advaita.

This inference of the Advaitin is from the Advaita work, the *Vivaraṇa*. It is urged to establish the positive nature of nescience. Jayatīrtha states the inference in full and points out the significance and function of the words therein. The function of the word "removable by itself" is to make it inapplicable to adṛṣṭa *i.e.*, unseen potency; unseen potency prevents the effect from coming into existence though the causes be present. So valid cognition cannot remove the unseen potency, because it prevents the rise of the said cognition itself. The words "present in its own locus" are used to avoid the applicability of the definition to cognisedness *i.e.*, jñātatā. The Bhāṭṭa school of Mīmāmsa recognises that cognition of an object is inferred from the cognisedness that is found in the objects cognised. This special quality is said to be generated in the object by the cognition at the momemt of the cognition. The attribute "cognisedness" is found in objects, and not in cognitions. So the words "present in its own locus" are used. Non-cognisedness is not present in the locus *i.e.*, valid cognition. Besides this, the aim of the Advaitin is to establish the positive nescience having for its substrate the ātman and that is secured by the use of the words " present in its own locus ".

The Dvaitin criticises the inference in detail. He points out that the said probandum is not definitely in the subjects. Valid cognition is the modification of the internal organ and as such it has for its material cause Manas. Manas is inert. According to the Advaitins of the Vivaraṇa school, an inert object cannot be the content or locus. The inconstancy of the probans is also urged. Besides, the attribute " being other than its own anterior non-existence " is urged to be purposeless. A positive entity does not destroy its own anterior non-existence. The coming into being of an entity alone destroys its anterior non-existence. Being other than its own anterior non-existence is said to be superfluous.

The inference is further criticised by questioning the nature of the entity said to precede the valid cognition. If it is real there is the defect of the establishment of the established, because, the Dvaitin admits that nescience is real. If it is said to be indeterminable, such indeterminability is not found in the example *i.e.*, " darkness preceding the light " ; darkness is not in the example ; there is thus the defect of the absence of the probandum.

If the Advaitin defines it as that which is not specified to be indeterminable or real, such a general description is not acceptable. No such common attribute is said to exist as between a validly cognised entity and an invalidly cognised entity. Indeterminability is not validly cognised because there is no pramāṇa securing its cognition. A common attribute is possible only as between two validly cognised objects. There cannot be any common attribute between the horns of a hare and the horns of a cow, because one of them is unreal and non-existent.

Further the definition of the probandum is applicable to demerit. Demerit is admitted to be destroyed by valid cognition. The commentator cites the example of the cancellation of our sins at the sight of the holy waters of Setu near Rāmesvaram. Demerit is there destroyed by cognition.

The Davitin criticises the probans of the inference *i.e.*, "being the manifestor of the non-manifested". The term manifestor is resolved to mean three alternatives. It does not mean the instrument of cognition. The sense-organ of sight is an instrument of cognition. In it there is the probans and not the probandum. Hence the inconstancy of the probans. Besides in the example *i.e.*, the light of a lamp as it first comes into existence from darkness, the light is not considered as an instrument of cognition. It is treated as an accessory to the instrument of cognition. It only destroys the obstruction *i.e.*, darkness. So in the example there is the defect of the absence of the probans. In the subject "valid cognitions" there is the absence of the probans *i.e.* being the instrument of cognition. Cognition cannot be the instrument of its own self. Hence the defect of the non-establishment of the probans in respect of the subject.

If the term "manifestor" means "the accessory to an instrument of cognition", there is the inconstancy of the probans in respect of collyrium (applied to the eyes). This collyrium is said to have the power of helping the eyes to see through darkness. So it is an accessory to the instrument of cognition. In it *i.e.*, the eye-paint, the probandum is not present. Hence the defect of the inconstancy of the probans. The term manifestor means "being cognition"; since in the example, *i.e.*, light, there is no jñātatvam there is the defect of the absence of the probans in respect of the example.

The Advaitin urges that experience is the Pramāṇa in respect of the positive nature of nescience. He points out that the recollection "I did not know anything" is the evidence for it. This recollection is from the man who has just got up from his sleep. The Dvaitin urges that the recollection has for its content the non-existence of cognition and not positive nescience. It cannot be so, says the Advaitin, because in deep sleep, as all the senses are at rest, there cannot be any knowledge. Further the cognition of non-existence is dependent on the cognition of the locus as well as the counter-correlate. In the absence of both the cognitions, the Dvaitin cannot hold that the content of the recollection is the non-existence of the cognition. The Dvaitin replies that witness-consciousness cognises the locus as well as the counter-correlate and hence the content of the recollection cognition is the non-existence of cognition. According to S'rī Madhva, Sākṣin is always awake. It is of the very nature of the self (svarūpa) unlike the other six sense organs (indriya), which are elemental. It is this sākṣin that cognises the locus as well as the counter-correlate.

The Advaitin cites another inference to prove the positive nature of nescience. The subject of the inference, nescience, is the non-existence of cognition: the probans is "being not cognised by the appropriate pramāṇa." There is the defect of the non-establishment of the probans. As nescience is said to be the non-existence of cognition, the probans, "being not cognised by any pramāṇa" is not there. Nescience is not cognised by pramāṇa, because it is destroyed by pramāṇa, like certain knowledge.

The Dvaitin criticises his inference as being inapplicable. Once we state that nescience is not cognised by pramāṇa, it is contradictory to state an inference to establish it. Inference being a pramāṇa cannot cognise nescience. Hence the inapplicability of the inference.

The Advaitin tries to get over this contradiction by positing the presence of the pervasion by psychosis and by negating the presence of the pervasion by cognition in which consciousness is reflected (phala). Through the positing of the cognition of the subject by psychosis the cognition for the subject is secured. Through the negation of the cognition of the fruit (the cognition in which consciousness is reflected) the defect of the non-establishment of the probans in respect of itself is refuted.

To this the Dvaitin replies that the Advaitin does not admit the pervasion by the psychosis of nescience. Nescience is destroyed by vṛtti-jñāna and it is beginningless, whereas the psychosis lasts only for some time; so it cannot be pervaded by it. Further the Dvaitin points out that the Advaitin's pervasion is vitiated in respect of impressions. The impressions are located in the manas. They produce recollection or recognition and after that they die away. Recognition destroys impression; so impressions are destroyed by the pramāṇa *i.e.*, recognition. Impressions are cognised by pramāṇa. "Not being cognised by pramāṇa" is the probandum. This is not present in impressions; but there is the probans *i.e.*, "being destroyed by pramāṇa". Hence the inconstancy in respect of impressions. Recognition according to Dvaita Vedānta is a pramāṇa that is subsumed under perception.

The Advaitin cites another pramāṇa from usage in support of the positive nature of nescience. It takes the following form "I know not the sense stated by you". Here the content of the cognition is positive nescience and it is not the non-existence of cognition. The content of the statement cannot be the non-existence of cognition. The cognition of non-existence is dependent on the cognition of the locus and the counter-correlate. The admission contradicts the sense of the usage in question *i.e.*, "I know not the sense stated by you". If he denies the need for cognition of the locus and counter-correlate, the absence of that prevents him from maintaining that the content of the statement is non-existence of cognition. So the Advaitin concludes that it is necessary to maintain that the content of the statement is positive nescience.

The siddhāntin resolves the usage "I know not the sense stated by you" to mean two things. Does it mean that every particular stated is restated and said to be not known, or does it mean that the thing in general is not known? It cannot be the first, because the moment we admit that this is a restatement of every particular, there would be impossibility for the usage. If the Advaitin further contends that there is such a usage, then the Dvaitin interprets the statement "I know not the sense stated by you" to mean "I know not the sense stated by you as valid." There is the cognition of the sense stated, but not the sense as valid. The content of the statement is the non-existence of the cognition as valid. The sense of a statement can be cognised as it is and at the same time be not cognised as valid. In a polemical debate the proponent first comprehends the sense stated by the opponent and refutes it after restating it.

The Advaitin maintains that the position maintained by the Dvaitin is self-contradictory. The usage "I know not (validly) the sense stated by you" is valid. This statement is a qualified cognition and its immediate content is non-existence of cognition. The content of the "that" of that cognition is some object. The Advaitin contends that the object of the second cognition is also the content of the original cognition, because it is an attribute of it. Once it becomes its content it is also urged to be valid. If that be valid there is contradiction of one's own words in the statement that what is known as valid is not so known.

The Dvaitin does not admit that the content of the second cognition is to be treated as the content of the original cognition. The content of the usage is what is immediately in touch with it, and not what is remotely connected with it.

The Dvaitin admits that the knowledge of the locus and the counter-correlate is necessary. He holds that it is known of the particular, first in a general way; and there is non-existence of the cognition. Such a position is unacceptable to the Advaitin, because it establishes that the content of the statement under discussion is non-existence of cognition. He may contend that if the particular is cognised, it is necessary for the cognition of its non-existence, because cognition of the counter-correlate is indispensable to it. Hence there is no possibility for the statement.

The Dvaitin retorts that we have at times a general knowledge that there is some particular. For instance we say that there is some particular point there. We do not know the nature of that particular, but still we refer to particulars from our general knowledge of them. Usage with reference to the particular is intelligible with the presupposition that we have some general knowledge of them. (For Advaitin's refutation of Dvaitins criticism. See *Advaitasiddhi*, p. 133).

XIII (131). It is pointed out that the Advaitin too has to adopt a position similar to that of the Dvaitin. The nescience which is considered to be positive must have a content. Was that content known earlier or unknown? If it be said that it is known, there is no possibility for usage of nescience in respect of it. We cannot be ignorant about what is known. If it be said that the content is not known earlier there is no possibility for the usage of nescience, because the cognition of nescience presupposes the knowledge of its content and locus. As against this position the Advaitin points out that all things whether as known or as unknown are contents for the witness-consciousness. The objects are cognised by witness-consciousness in a general way prior to the vṛtti-jñāna and the usage "I know not the sense stated by you." If it be said and contended that though the sense is established by witness-consciousness still the desire to know the pramāṇa for it is sufficient reason for the usage, it is not so, says the siddhāntin. For a thing that is established by witness-consciousness, the desire to make known a pramāṇa is fruitless. The Advaitin has to admit like the Dvaitin that what is cognised in general is restated with a desire to know the particular. There is no valid instrument of knowledge for the Advaitin to establish the positive nature of nescience. The non-establishment of the nature of nescience leads logically to the non-establishment of its effect. Hence the refutation of the positive nature of nescience on account of its unintelligible nature.

XIV (132, 133). The seventh and the last of the Advaitin's definitions of illusoriness is, "being cognised in the same locus as its own absolute non-existence". If the term "absolute non-existence" in the definition means "asat", then the definition of mithyātva applies only to asat. Such a position is opposed to the Advaitin's view that the world is neither asat nor sat. If the term "absolute non-existence" means something other than existence *i.e.*, being indeterminable as real or unreal, such a thing does not exist at all. Hence the non-establishment of the probandum. If it is contended that the term under discussion means "being other than real" that turns out to be unreal; hence the adduced defect is not got over. There is no middle ground between the real and the unreal.

XV (134-142). The first of the probans is taken up for criticism. The probans cognisability is resolved to mean two things: (1) the object of cognition and (2) non-self-luminosity. (See *Tattva-pradīpikā*, p. 34.) The first alternative again is resolved into two: (1) is the cognition of the nature of psychosis or (2) is it of the nature of consciousness? If it is the first, there is the defect of the inconstancy of the probans in respect of the Ātman. The probandum mithyātva is not found in the Ātman and the probans cognisability is found in it. The Ātman is the object of the psychosis generated by the study of Vedānta. The Advaitin further contends that in the Ātman there is not that cognisability which is in the form of the fruit of cognition. There is then the discussion as to what the term, fruit, means; is it cognisedness or empirical usage? If it is cognisedness it is not present even in objects of cognition. Cognisedness according to the Mīmāṁsakas is present only in the objects present, and not in the destroyed and past ones. Hence the defect of the non-establishment of the probans. There is also the defect of partial non-establishment of the probans in respect of the subject. The destroyed, future, and eternally to be inferred objects have no cognisedness, because cognisedness can only form a part of the subject; hence the defect.

If the Advaitin contends that the destroyed, future and eternally to be inferred objects have cognisedness, the Dvaitin points out that such a position is opposed to the Advaita school of thought. In support of it, the Dvaitin quotes a passage from Citsukha who, while defining self-luminosity, points out that the definition should not include the destroyed, future, and eternally to be inferred objects. In order to achieve their exclusion he used the phrase "capacity to be the object of empirical usage of immediacy." Else, because there is no cognisedness in them they too would be self-luminous. Hence it follows that there is no cognisedness in them. So the defect of partial non-establishment of the probans in the subject stands.

If the term "phala" means *empirical usage* there is again the defect of inconclusiveness of the probans in respect of the Ātman, because the Ātman is an object of the empirical usage arising from psychosis. If the cognition is said to be in the form of consciousness the Dvaitin does not admit it in the object like the pot etc., which form a part of the subject. Hence the defect of partial non-establishment in respect of the subject. (For a refutation of Dvaita criticism, see *Advaitasiddhi*, p. 10.)

XVI (143-146). The second definition of cognisability is examined in detail and criticised. It is defined as the non-existence of self-luminosity. Self-luminosity is defined as "not being an object of cognition"; its non-existence, cognisability, turns out to mean "being an object of cognition". Such a position has been already criticised. The defects urged in there holds good in this case also.

Self-luminosity may be defined as that cognition which does not depend on any consciousness other than itself for the empirical usage in respect of itself. The non-existence of it would be cognisability. Then there is the defect of the inconstancy of the probans in respect of the Ātman. The Cognition of the Ātman as non-dual, self-luminous etc., is dependent on the psychosis generated by scriptural statements like "One only without the second". Thus there is cognisability in the Ātman and there is the non-existence of the probandum. Hence the inconstancy of the probans.

The Advaitin contends that the probans is not inconstant in respect of the indeterminate cognition of the Ātman. Such an indeterminate cognition is not dependent on any consciousness other than itself. By the indeterminate usage is meant a thing which is neither real nor unreal, *i.e.*, cognising a thing as neither real nor unreal. The Dvaitin points out that the objects like pot also can be treated likewise. The Advaitin does not accept that there is indeterminate usage in respect of objects like pot etc. To this the Dvaitin replies that similarly let there be no indeterminate usage in respect of the Ātman, too.

The Advaitin instances the experience of the self in deep sleep as the evidence for indeterminate usage. The Dvaitin does not admit that in deep sleep the self is indeterminate. The individual after a good sleep recollects that he had sound and enjoyable sleep. The attributes "*sound*" and "*enjoyable*" must have characterised it. So in deep sleep the self is not indeterminate as the Advaitin holds.

XVII (147-151). There is another definition of self-luminosity by Citsukha *i.e.*, "it is the capacity to be the object of empirical usage while not being an object of cognition." This definition is said to be contradictory, because that which is not cognised can never become an object of cognition and there will be no usage about it. The definition is impossible. Granting that the definition is somehow not contradictory, still there is the need for clearing the definition of self-luminosity which is a complex one. Its opposite is cognisability. The non-existence of a complex character can result in one of the three ways, (1) by the non-existence of the qualification *i.e.*, the attribute (2) by the non-existence of the substrate or (3) by the non-existence of both. If it results through the non-existence of the attribute, "not being an object of cognition" may itself be the probans. Defects of the position have already been noted.

If it be the non-existence of the substrate, then there is the defect of the non-establishment of the probans in respect of the subject. The probans is not present in the subject; its non-existence alone is present. Objects like pot etc., are objects of empirical usage of immediacy. The probans is "not being objects of empirical usage of immediacy". Hence the defect of partial non-establishment. Though the probans be treated as present in merit and demerit which are said to be not the objects of empirical usage of immediacy, still the Dvaitin contends that even merit and demerit are objects of mind's perception which appears in the form of recollection. So they too are objects of empirical usage in the whole subject of immediacy. Hence the defect is non-establishment of the probans and not partial non-establishment of the probans in respect of the subject.

The manas is accepted by the Dvaitin as a separate Karaṇa. It has two functions. It cognises all external objects through the instrumentality of all other senses. Its independent function is to be the pramāṇa in respect of recollection. It is this special function that makes the Dvaitin admit the independent nature of mind as a karaṇa.

If the non-existence be of the attribute, there is the defect that the substrate has no function for it. Besides the substrate is non-established.

XVIII (152-179). The cognisability referred to by the Dvaitin can be neither of the valid nor of the delusive type. If it is said to be of the valid type it is opposed to Advaita. If it is said to be of the delusive type it is not accepted by the Dvaitin. The probans in a valid inference must be acceptable to both the disputants. Hence neither of the alternatives is established. The Advaitin finds a way out of the difficulty and contends that the probans is defined in general terms and not in a specific manner. Besides, he points out that it is not right to analyse into specific particulars a probans defined in general terms and thus refute it. Such a procedure would lead to the total non-existence of all inferences. In the ordinary inference where we establish fire with the help of the probans "smoke," if some one were to ask us as to what exactly is the probans, whether the smoke that is related to the present place and time or smoke that is related to some other place and time, we cannot give any answer. If we hold the smoke related to the present place and time to be the probans, then such a probans is not established in the subject. Thus there would be no valid inference.

The Dvaitin answers in detail. The inference which establishes fire with the help of the probans, smoke, has for its probans the smoke defined in general terms. It is by itself able to establish fire. So there is no need for the analysis of the probans, smoke into particular kinds. The particular kinds of smoke have no function in inference.

It is not so in the case of the probans, cognisability. There is no common attribute between delusive cognisability and valid cognisability. A comparison is instituted to illustrate this point. There is no common attribute, lotusness, present in the sky-lotus and lake-lotus. The sky-lotus, just like the delusive cognisability, is non-existent. Then how is it that we speak of delusive cognisability? It is just like the reference to the sky-lotus and nothing better.

Besides, the probans is contradictory, because it is found in places where there is no probandum *i.e.*, illusoriness. In the Ātman there is no illusoriness but there is cognisability. It is only found in the real *i.e.*, Ātman. This contradiction is sought to be refuted on the ground that cognisability is found in the shell-silver also. There the cognition is of shell only and not of the silver, says the Dvaitin. The question as to how shell can be the content of silver-cognition has to be answered. The Dvaitin resolves the term silver-cognition to mean two things: (1) the cognition that has silver, for its content, (2) the cognition that has the form of silver. It cannot be the first because there is no silver in the shell. It is the cognition that has the form of silver. The shell-silver-cognition has for its content shell; owing to defect it cognises the form of silver. Further such cognisability is not found in the subject.

The probans cognisability is criticised by the Dvaitin and he points out that it is inconstant, because it is present in the Atman where there is no probandum *i.e.*, illusoriness. The Advaitin contends that the Ātman is not cognised. To say that the

Ātman is not cognised is self-contradiction. We cannot affirm an attribute or negate an attribute, when we do not know the substrate. The statement that Ātman is not cognised implies that Atman must have cognisability. Without such an implication the denial is of no meaning. Hence the self-contradiction of the Advaitin's statement.

The Dvaitin, in support of the cognisability of the Ātman, cites two inferences. The first inference has for its probandum cognisability and the probans is "being a thing". The defect of the non-establishment of the probans in respect of the subject is likely to be urged. The subject *i.e.*, the Ātman is not a thing. Hence the Dvaitin states a second inference which is not open to the said defect. The cognisability of the self is established in a round-about way by this inference. This pot is other than that cognisable which is different from that world that is other than this pot plus self. The example is any other pot, say X, this pot being "Y plus the self Z". X is different from Y; Z is a cognisable entity which is other than the world different from Y+Z; thus by implication cognisability of Z is secured.

The expression Brahman-knowledge points out that Brahman is the content of the cognition. Brahman-knowledge is not possible without Brahman being the content. The genitive case points out that Brahman is the content. The Advaitins contend that Brahman-knowledge means knowledge whose form is Brahman. That contention is dismissed after examining the several meanings of the term "form". The Dvaitin concludes that Brahman is an object of cognition and is cognised. Thus the adduced inconstancy of the probans, cognisability, in respect of Brahman is maintained.

XX (188-200). The second probans "inertness" is taken up for criticism and declared to be defective. Inertness is resolved into four alternatives: (1) If inertness is construed as "not being the substrate of cognition", there is the defect of the partial non-establishment of the probans in respect of the subject. The subject includes the empirical Ātmans. These Ātmans are substrates of cognition. Hence the non-existence of the probans in this part of the subject. Besides there is the inconstancy of the probans also. It is found in Ātman and in absolute non-existence, places where the probandum is not found.

(2) If inertness means "not being self-hood", it is not very clear. This definition means one of two things: (1) being different from Ātman or (2) not being the substrate of self-hood. The former alternative is not accepted by the Advaitin. According to them there is no world apart from Brahman. In fact there is nothing apart from Brahman. Whatever appears as apart from Brahman is only an illusory manifestation of Brahman. If it be contended that though there is no object really different from Brahman, there is the phenomenally different object, such a position is not admitted by the Dvaitin. The probans must be acceptable to both the disputants in a discussion. Besides, the probans is inconstant in respect of absolute non-existence. In absolute non-existence there is no probandum, but there is the probans "being different from the Ātman". Hence the inconstancy.

(3) If "inertness" means "not being a substrate of self-hood" such a position is already criticised. In sections (16-23) the several alternative definitions of self-hood are examined and they are found to be tainted by one of three defects, (1) non-distinction from probandum, (2) non-establishment of the probans, (3) inconstancy of the probans.

(4) If inertness means "being the form of ajñāna" there is the defect of partial non-establishment in respect of the cognition in the form of psychosis. This forms a part of the subject. And in it there is non-existence of the probans *i.e.*, the form of ajñāna. Is it the form of cognition or is it cognition itself? Such a position is not easy to maintain. A Cognition must have a content. When we refer to Ātman as cognition, what is the content in that cognition? It cannot be Ātman itself: then there would be no difference between the content and cognition. The content of a

cognition and the cognition cannot be identical. Such a position is contradictory. The content of the cognition cannot be any other entity. (For Advaitins refutation of Dvaita criticism, See *Advaita siddhi*, p. 13.)

XXI (201-210). The Dvaitin criticises the third and the last probans of the Advaitin, namely, " finitude ". The term " finitude ", is analysed to mean three things: (1) spatial finitude, (2) temporal finitude, (3) difference. If it is the first, there is the defect of partial non-establishment of the probans in respect of the subject. Time and Ākās'a form a part of the subject though they are divisible into parts. The Aṁs'ikāla is not particularised. It does not admit of divisions. So also the non-elemental Ākās'a. In Time and in Ākās'a there is the absence of the probans " spatial finitude ". Hence the defect. If the probans means " temporal finitude ", even then there is the same defect, because the probans is not preseet in Ākās'a and in Time.

The Advaitin may contend that everything other than Brahman has spatial and temporal finitude and that there is in this way the establishment of the probans in Time and Akās'a; hence the absence of the contradiction. The Dvaitin urges that the contradiction is not removed. The term spatial finitude means " being the counter-correlate of absolute non-existence located in some place." When the Advaitin declares that everything has spatial finitude, in order to make intelligible the spatial finitude there must be the counter-correlate. Such a counter-correlate forms a part of the subject. Hence spatial finitude cannot be established. If another counter-correlate outside the world be admitted, there is the defect of partial non-establishment of the probans in respect of that counter-correlate. Hence the defect of contradiction. The Advaitin then contends that the Brahman is the counter-correlate, because everything is super-imposed on it. These objects are denied there. With Brahman as the counter-correlate finitude can be attributed to Kāla and Ākās'a. Hence there is no contradiction.

The Dvaitin points out that the Advaitin's definition of finitude means sublatability. If sublatability is the probans there is the defect of non-difference of the probans and the probandum. The probandum illusoriness is defined as the sublatable. Hence the defect.

The Dvaitin in criticising temporal finitude which is the second alternative, points out the same defect as in the case of spatial finitude. The defect is contradiction. Then the question as to what exactly is the pramāṇa that establishes temporal finitude in Ākāśa and Time is taken up. It cannot be the probans "intertness". The probans intertness is already refuted. If according to Advaita the temporal finitude present in objects like pot are due to inertness, the Dvaitin objects to it and attributes the temporal finitude therein to an adjunct *i.e.* "being an effect". The pervasion is not invariable. The probans is inconstant in respect of nescience. Nescience is not an effect but is inert. Hence the inconstancy. If nescience be said to be an effect there is self-contradiction. Throughout Advaita literature nescience is spoken of as beginningless. There is no cause for it; so it cannot be an effect.

The term "temporal finitude" is resolved to mean three things: (1) being non-eternal, (2) having a beginning, (3) not being in all three times. If we accept the first alternative there is the inconstancy of the probans, "inertness" in respect of mokṣa. Mokṣa is eternal. So there is the non-existence of the probandum "being non-eternal". There is the probans, "inertness" there. Hence the defect. The description of mokṣa as the fifth form is not without its significance. The inconstancy of the probans must be pointed out outside the subject. In order to secure the exclusion from the subject, mokṣa is defined as the fifth. (1) It is not real, (2) nor is unreal, (3) nor is it real and unreal because such a concept violates the law of contradiction (4) nor is it indeterminable. Exclusion from the indeterminable results from mokṣa=destruction of avidyā, where avidyā itself is indeterminable. Mention of the fifth prakāra view is to exclude these, according to whom mokṣa is ātma-svarūpa; in such a case mokṣa is sat or cit, not jaḍa; if however it is of a fifth form, it must be jaḍa. If mokṣa is said to be characterised by temporal finitude, there is contradiction for the words of the Advaitin who maintains non-return. (For the Advaitin's refutation of the criticism, see *Advaita siddhi*, p. 15.)

XXII (211-218). The term temporal finitude is interpreted as "being the substrate of reciprocal non-existence." "Being the substrate of reciprocal non-existence" is just another name for difference. If temporal finitude is difference, the scriptural statements like "neti—neti" declare that Brahman is different from the world. Thus the probans is inconstant in respect of Brahman. The probandum, "illusoriness" is not present and the probans, "being a substrate of reciprocal non-existence" is there. Hence the defect. If the difference predicated by the scriptures be said to be phenomenal *i.e.*, the difference resulting from nescience, the Dvaitin does not admit that. Then the probans would be "real difference". The probans, "real difference" is not established in respect of the subject, becauese the subject is illusory. Besides, the same probans can establish the reality of the universe. The form of the inference will be as follows. "The world under dispute is not illusory, because it is the substrate of real reciprocal non-existence." For in the self which is different from the unreal there is real difference: nacre-silver, though illusory, does not possess real difference.

The Dvaitin urges that perception sublates the truth of the Advaitin's inference. Perception warrants that the object of cognition is real. Then there is an examination of the term real. It is resolved to mean six different things. The acceptance of any of the first five alternatives does not lead us on to the contradiction of the Advaitin's inference by perception. The sixth alternative *i.e.*, being real=unsublatability, is not accepted by the Advaitin. Perception has not the necessary capacity to apprehend what is in the future. Perception can comprehend what is present and immediate. Perception cannot comprehend the non-existence of the sublation located in the future. If it be held that perception can do so, then the reality of such a perception will be on a par with the reality of the *fata morgana* (the mythical city of the gandharvas).

The Dvaitin admits that perception has a capacity to comprehend the non-existence of the sublation in the future. This is clear by its very capacity to cognise the non-sublatability in the present. But there is an essential difference between the two perceptions. Validity according to Madhva is intrinsic and invalidity is extrinsic. The validity present in cognition is produced as well as ascertained by the very instruments which produce and ascertain the cognition. The instruments that originate the cognition originate its validity. The Cognition and its validity are manifested by witness-consciousness. As for invalidity it is originated by the defects associated with the instruments of knowledge. The Sākṣin cognises the cognition aspect of the invalid cognition and invalidity in it is inferred. Invalidity is extrinsic. The perception of the mythical city of the gandharvas is invalid because in it there is the defect "non-existence." The cognition of unsublatability is established because there is a defect undermining it. Hence the difference.

XXIII (219-224). The Advaitin argues that inference sublates the knowledge derived through perception. The Siddhāntin points out that inference cannot sublate perception, because inference is dependent on perception. If inference be said to have the capacity to sublate perception, then the perception of heat in fire can be sublated by the inference that establishes the cold nature of fire. Such a conclusion is abusurd on the face of it. Inference as such has no capacity to refute the content of perception. Inference is not an independent pramāṇa like perception or verbal testimony. The cognition derived through perception cannot be sublated by a perception of equal strength, let alone of inference. (See *Advaita siddhi*, p. 28.)

The Advaitin points out an inference, where inference sublates perception. The perception of the colour of the sky gives us the impression that it is blue. This is refuted by the inference "the sky is not blue, because it is incorporeal." The cognition of the colour of the sky is due to verbal testimony and not due to inference. The Advaitins frame an inference to refute the validity of the perception. "Perception which is under dispute is delusive cognition, because it is a perception, like the perception of the non-existent mythical city of the gandharvas." The Dvaitin frames a counter-inference in order to occasion the undesirable. It is as follows. "The vedic statements with reference to Brahman that it is existence, knowledge etc. are invalid, because they are statements like the meaningless statements about an aged ox." The adduced invalidty of the vedic statements is not acceptable to the Advaitin. The term perception has to be explained. If it is interpreted to mean the semblance of perception, there is the absence of such an entity in the subject. Hence the non-establishment of the probans. If it is said to be valid perception such an entity is not present in the example. If it is defined as mere knowledge there is over-pervasion of the probans in respect of the cognition generated by Vedic statements like "knowledge, existence bliss" etc.

XXIV (225-235). The Advaitin's inference establishing the illusory nature of the universe is contradicted by scriptures. The mantra in the Ṛgveda, II-24-12 is cited as an instance for it. This mantra predicates reality of the universe. The reality predicated by the scripture, the Advaitin holds, is phenomenal, The Dvaitin argues that it is futile to declare phenomenal reality because nobody disputes it. So scripture predicates absolute reality because it has to refute the position popularly held by the Advaitins, namely, the ascription of phenomeual reality to the universe.

The Advaitin urges that scriptural statements like "there are no differents whatsoever here" negate the reality explained by statements that "the universe is real". The scriptural statements that ascribe reality to the universe are modes of restatement which are refuted by other scriptural statements that deny reality to the universe. As against this position the Dvaitin points out that the reverse of what the Advaitin holds is the truth. There is nothing to prevent us from explaining scriptural statements like "there are no differents whatsoever here" as restating the unreality of differences and that scriptural statements like "universe is real" as refuting them. It is possible at this rate to hold that scriptural statements like "there was non-existence in the beginning" refute the statements like "the Brahman is knowledge and infinitude". Before restating and refuting a position there is the need to establish it through a pramāṇa other than scripture. The Dvaitin points out that the illusoriness of the universe is established by the probans, "cognisability" and the reality of Brahman has to be the substrate of delusion. Delusion is not accountable otherwise than on the assumption of Brahman as the substrate.

The reality of the world cognised, is it an object of valid cognition or not? It cannot be an object of valid cognition, because what is a content of a valid cognition cannot be refuted. The Advaitin does not admit validity for what is negated. It cannot be the object of an invalid cognition, because that which is not established cannot be restated. Besides, whenever there is a restatement of a fact it takes the following form "what they say," even where such a form is absent. There is some special reason to justify the ascribed repetitiveness. Thus in "kill not a Brahmin", Brahmanicide due to natural hatred is said to be restated for the sake of a prohibition, though the form of the test is not "what is established by lust or hate *viz.*, brahmanicide, that should be avoided". The special ground for this treatment is that the proximity to a negation can only be of the already established; and in respect of this element there can be only a restatment.

XXV (236, 237). The Dvaitin points out the contradiction for the Advaitin's inference by a verse in the Gītā (XVI-8). 'In the 16th Chapter there is the classification of men into two types, the devas and the asuras (demonic tempered men). There is a detailed and eloquent description of demonic tempered men. They never reach my feet says the Lord Kṛṣna. The men of āsuric temper hold that the universe is unreal and that is has no substrate. They say that there is no Īs'vara. Hence the opposition of the smṛti to the Advaitin's position.

If the Advaitin contends that the unreality predicated with reference to the world in the Gitā verse is not absolute unreality, the Dvaitin replies that there is no disputant who holds such a position. If the Advaitin seeks to point out that the Buddhist holds that the universe is absolutely unreal, it is not so says Madhva; since even the s'ūnyavādin admits empirical reality called samvṛta-sattva.

XXVI (238-252). The Dvaitin states his inference to prove the reality of the universe. The inference is as follows. "The universe under dispute is real, because it is an object of valid knowledge, like Brahman". A detailed examination of the formal correctness of the limbs of the inference is undertaken. The probandum of the inference is clearly stated. It is reality *i.e.*, being unsublatable. The probans "being an object of pramāṇa" is resolved to mean two things: (1) being an object of the pramāṇa that makes known the real or (2) being the object of the pramāṇa that makes known the phenomenal. It cannot be the first alternative, because the Advaitins do not admit that pramāṇas like perception can make known what is real. Nor can it be admitted that pramāṇas like perception can make known the phenomenal, because it is not acceptable to the Dvaitin. To know a thing through a pramāṇa and then say that it makes known the phenomenal is contradiction in terms. Pramāṇa always makes known what is real. Further the example *i.e.*, Brahman, is devoid of the probans *i.e.*, "being an object of pramāṇa." (For Advaitin's refutation of criticism, see *Advaita siddhi*, p. 64.)

The Dvaitin holds that there is no pramāṇa to establish the fact that pramāṇas like perception do not cognise the real. The

Dvaitin states an inference to prove that a pramāṇa like perception does make known the real, because it is a pramāṇa, like "reality knowledge." After establishing the fact that perception makes known the real, the Dvaitin goes to prove the reality of the universe. "The universe is an object of a pramāṇa that makes known the real, because it is an entity other than the content of a delusive cognition." The Dvaitin says that the inference is not vitiated by the adjunct self-hood.

XXVII (253-260). The Dvaitin puts forward a second probans to establish the reality of the universe. That probans is examined in detail. Practical efficiency (arthakriyākāritva) is the probans. The Advaitin urges that this probans is inconstant in respect of the enjoyment of a fair damsel in dream. The dream-damsel is unreal; but still the dream effects certain physiological reactions.

The Dvaitin points out that the instance cited is similar to the subject and that the inconstancy of the probans should be pointed out only in places other than the subject and those similar to the subject. The Advaitin points out that the probans is inconstant in respect of the fear generated by rope which is delusively cognised as the snake. The point is that though it is unreal, it still has the probans "fruitfulness". The Dvaitin in reply points out that what generates fear is not the delusively cognised snake, but the cognition itself. It is the cognition that is responsible for the fear. Those who maintain that the delusive object is the cause of terror in men cannot account for the absence of terror in men who have no knowledge of the harmful objects near them. From this it follows that what generates fear is the cognition of the object and not the object. (For the Advaitin's answer, see *Advaita siddhi*, p. 68.) If it is the cognition that gives rise to terror, does it by itself gives rise to terror or with its content? If it by itself gives rise to fear then there is the possibility that all cognitions could do so. If with its contents it gives rise to fear, then the snake too is responsible for the fear.

The Dvaitin makes out that the rope which is cognised as the snake is the content of the cognition. It is not the snake that generates fear. Hence there is no inconstancy of the probans. The example of the inference is criticised *i.e.*, Ātman. The probans fruitful activity is said to be not present in the Ātman. The Dvaitin refutes that and points out that there are many scriptural statements whose purport is Ātman as the cause of the world. The Ātman is said to be the creator, destroyer, etc., of this universe. So the example Ātman is not devoid of the probans.

If the Advaitin urges that the Ātman which has fruitful activity is included in the subject, then there is no difference between nihilistic Buddhism and Advaita in respect of denying the self. If it is further urged by the Advaitin that he admits an Ātman which is other than the one included in the subject and that hence his position is not the same as that of the Buddhists the Dvaitins reply that the attribute "being other than" is an attribute enough to secure the inclusion of the Ātman in the subject. Besides, the fruitful activity present in the qualified Ātman is bound to be present even in the Ātman transcending the qualified cognition.

The Dvaitin puts forward a third probans for the establishment of the reality of the universe. The same difficulties that were urged in the case of the last probans can also be urged in the present case.

XXVIII (261). The Dvaitin urges an adjunct to vitiate the Advaitin's inference. The adjunct is "being the content of a cognition that is generated by a defect." This adjunct is present wherever there is the probandum. Both the adjunct and the probandum are found in the shell-silver. The probans is not co-pervasive with the adjunct. The adjunct is not present in the subject and the probans is there. The adduced defect satisfies the definition of an adjunct.

As against this if the Advaitin urges that he would establish the presence of the adjunct in the subject, the Dvaitin holds that such a position is defective. Further illusoriness alone being in question, there will be the defect of arthāntaratā. The text may also mean that in establishing doṣagamyatva, because of cognisability, there are as many defects as in establishing illusoriness with the same probans.

XXIX (262-265). The example in the Advaitin's inference is criticised as being devoid of the probandum. The probandum "indeterminability," or "being nescience or a product thereof" is not present in the shell-silver. The Advaitin holds that it is present there. In the inference, "shell-silver" has some cause, because it is occasional (*i.e.*, not constant) like pot. The shell-silver is not a product of what is real or unreal; so it must be by exclusion a product of nescience.

The Dvaitin examines the probans "being occasional". Does it mean "being cognised at some time?" There is in this case the non-existence of the pervasion in respect of Atman and Akās'a which, though eternal, are only cognised for some time. If it means "being born at some time" there is the non-establishment of the probans in the subject. The probandum is "possession of a cause." This has to be proved. The probans "being born at some time" is the same as the probandum. When that is not established this is also not established. Hence the non-establishment of the probans. The author concludes that all the three inferences stated by the Advaitin turn out to be invalid.

XXX (266-270). As against the Advaitin the Dvaitin urges a reductio ad absurdum. The antecedent of the hypothetical inference is "If the universe is illusory, the consequent is the acceptance of two real universes." The consequent which is not desirable to the Advaitin results as follows. Delusion pre-supposes the existence of two factors, the substrate and the achetype. Without these two factors delusion is impossible in any case. These two factors must be real and similar to the contents of the delusion. So the moment we accept the delusion there is the necessity to admit two real entities. The Advaitin is out to disprove the reality of one universe; so it is not acceptable to him to admit the reality of two. (For the Advaitin's answer to this see *Advaitasiddhi*, p. 95.)

The vyāpaka (pervader) is the prior existence of a substrate and archetype, and being illusory is the pervaded. The pervader is not present in the subject of the inference *i.e.*, the universe. So the law of parsimony requires us to accept the reality of this universe than the addmission of the reality of two universes.

XXXI (271-294). The Dvaitin proves the non-illusory nature of the universe with the help of two probans *i.e.*, (1) because it has no substrate, (2) because it has no archetype. These two are necessary for delusion, and without them we cannot account for delusion. The Advaitin points out that the probans is inconstant in respect of dream-objects. The objects seen in dream are illusory and they have no substrate. The probandum "illusoriness" is there, but the probans "having a substrate" is not there. The Advaitin elaborately sets forth his arguments to prove the illusory nature of dream objects. The dream objects cannot be beginningless and eternal. If they be so, we must all be able to cognise them before and after the dream cognition. We are not able to do so. If they are said to be born and destroyed then and there, it is a very unsound position. There is no material and efficient cause for the production of dream objects. It cannot be inside the body, because huge objects like elephants, mountains, etc., cannot get into the body. If the objects are said to be outside, then it must be visible to all others that are next to the dreamer. It is not so. Besides there is no sense-organ which can cognise the dream objects. It cannot be the outer sense-organs; for all of them rest in sleep. It cannot be mind, because mind cannot cognise outside objects independently. It needs the help of outer sense-organs. There is no substrate for dream objects. The Ātman cannot be the substrate of the dream objects. For a thing to be the substrate of the object it must not be cognised as different from the illusory object. The Ātman is cognised as different from the illusory object. When we see an elephant in a dream, we never say "I am the elephant." We cognise the "I" as different from the elephant.

The Dvaitin states that dream-objects are real and not illusory. So in dream-objects there is the non-existence of the probandum and there is also the non-existence of the probans. Thus there is no inconstancy of the probans in respect of dream-objects. The material cause of dream objects is the impressions (vāsana). The impressions of all our past experiences are deposited in the manas and not in the Atman. The bundle of impressions stored in manas constitutes the material cause of dream-objects. The efficient cause of the dream-objects is God. The authority for this is the *Vedānta* sūtra "God creats dream objects in dream states" (III. ii. 1). If it be contended that super-sensible cause alone can produce a super-sensible effect, the Dvaitin denies it. Eor example the two primal atoms constitute a binary atom, and three binary atoms go to make up a triad. Anything less than the triad is not seen. The binary and primal atoms though super-sensible still produce the cognisable triad. In the same way dream-objects too can be cognised though they are produced by a super-sensible material cause. Thus the reality of dream-objects is established.

The Advaitin criticises the probans of the Dvaitin's inference *i.e.*, "not having a substrate". This is pointed out to be non-established. The Ātman is the substrate of the world-illusion. As against this contention, the Dvaitin points out that the Ātman cannot be treated as the substrate. In any illusion the substrate is cognised as non-different from the super-imposed object. If it is cognised as different, there is no possibility for delusion at all. In the shell-silver delusion, if the individual cognised the shell as distinct from silver, there would be no delusion at all. As the Ātman is cognised as different from the world it cannot be its substrate. Besides, the universe and the Ātman have contrary qualities. In a delusion there must be certain similar qualities between the super-imposed object and the substrate; we never mistake the shell to be a tiger. Between two contrary objects, the relation of substrate and super-imposition is not possible. The super-imposition of the world on the Ātman is as unimaginable as the super-imposition of the mustard seeds on a mountain. The Advaitin criticises the second probans put forward by the Dvaitin to refute the illusory nature of the universe. The brobans is " not having an archetype ". The archetype of each illusory universe is its prior illusory universe. Thus the probans is shown to be non-existent there. The Dvaitin points out that the prior illusory universes are not real. The archetype must be real. Hence the probans is established.

XXXII (295-297). The Advaitin states a new inference to establish the illusory nature of the universe. This inference is from Citsukha's *Tattvapradīpikā*, p. 40. The subject of this inference is " this cloth " and the probandum is " being the counter-correlate of the non-existence present in these threads ". The probans is " being a whole." The cloth which is made out of these threads cannot be present elsewhere. If its existence is denied in the threads, it proves to be nowhere though it is seen. Its being seen and not being present in the threads leads us to the conclusion that it is illusory. Once cloth is proved to be so, in the same manner the whole world is proved to be illusory.

The Dvaitin criticises the inference and points out the following defects: (1) sublation by perception, (2) establishment of the established, (3) establishment of other than the intended and (4) partial non-establishment of the probandum. The absolute non-existence present in the threads cannot have any counter-correlate; perception points out the presence of the cloth in the thread. Hence the sublation.

The probandum *i.e.*, absolute non-existence of the cloth in the threads, is accepted by the Dvaitin. The threads and the cloth are in the relation of cause and effect. Cause and effect are non-different. The cloth and the threads are in a relation of the support and the supported. The threads are the supporters and the cloth is the supported. Both cannot be identical. Hence the defect.

If the probandum be worded "not being the effect of these threads" it yields a meaning other than the one intended by the Advaitin. The intended meaning is that the cloth is illusory. The present probandum points out that cloth is not an effect *i.e.*, it is eternal or that it is an effect of another set of threads. Hence the defect. Further the probans is not present in objects like Ākāśa which are not wholes. Thus there is partial non-establishment of the probans.

XXXIII (298-311). The probans "being a whole" (aṁśitva) of the Advaitin is sublated by perception. Perception points out that the cloth is in the threads. The Dvaitin resolves the probandum "being the counter-correlate of the absolute non-existence present in the threads" to mean one of two things, (1) either the non-existence of the cloth or (2) the non-existence of relation between the cloth and the threads. The first meaning is unacceptable to the Advaitin because he does not admit that the cloth is asat; he holds that it is indeterminable. If the Advaitin urges as against this that there is only a denial of the reality of the cloth and not the affirmation of its non-existence, the Dvaitin replies that there is no middle ground between the real and the unreal.

The phrase "being in the thread" is pointed out to be futile because it does not serve any purpose. The purpose may be said to be to avoid the defect of the establishment of the established, since on the logician's view, this cloth is the counter-correlate of the absolute non-existence present in another set of threads. But this is not acceptable to us since we do not at all admit absolute non-existence of this cloth; otherwise the cloth would be unreal (asat).

Again in the example *i.e.*, "another cloth" the probandum is non-existent. The Advaitin turns round and points out that if the probandum is denied its non-existence is affirmed. The affirmation leads to the fact of the presence of another cloth in these threads, which is a part of the subject. Such a deduction is not acceptable to the Dvaitin. The prior question is repeated *i.e.*, what is it that it means; is the relationship with cloth deduced, or the cloth itself? The first alternative does not hold good because there is no pervasion as a matter of fact. The pervasion should be of the form "wherever there is not the absolute non-existence of X there is relationship to X". But the Dvaitin does not affirm the latter (say relationship to cowness), even when he denies absolute non-existence (say cowness in the horse). This saṁsargābhāva has to be admitted even by the opponent in cases like the non-existence of the non-existence of cloth; else there would be self-dependence in the case of the non-existence of the cloth; for in this case, the alleged pervasion would be of the form "where cloth is not, there exists relationship to non-existence of cloth"; and that is absurd. Hence the alleged pervasion fails.

In the second case there is the defect of the establishment of the established, since even another cloth may be present in those threads through saṁyoga. The probandum worded a little differently fares no better. The probandum is worded as follows; "this cloth is not born out of these threads". If it is so worded there is the defect of non-establishment of the probans *i.e.*, "being a whole." That which is not an effect cannot be a whole. If that probans is said to be ultimately not real such a position is already refuted.

As for the defect of sublation by perception, the Advaitin points out that inference can sublate and invalidate the truth established by perception. For example the perception of the blue colour of the sky is sublated by the inference which establishes the colourless nature of the sky with the help of the probans "grossness". Likewise the reality of the cloth cognised through perception is sublated by inference with "being a whole" as the probans.

The Dvaitin refutes this position from two points of view. The sublation of the perceptive cognition of the blueness of the sky is not by inference; it is due to scripture. So inference does not sublate it. Besides, the very probans which is urged to establish the colourless nature of the sky may establish that Ākāśa (sky) is not the abode of sound. If it be urged that scripture sublates such a position, the same scripture establishes the colourless nature of the sky. There is no need for inference at all. If it be contended that the sublating pramāṇa must be accepted as valid by both the disputants, then there is nothing to deny the validity of the perception that cognises the cloth.

XXXV (328-330). Difference is the very nature of the things. It is an external fact. It is not an attribute that is present between two relata. For example A and B are different. According to Madhva the difference of A from B is not the same as the difference of B from A. Both the differences are different. They have different counter-correlates. (For the Advaitins answer to this criticism, see *Advaita siddhi*, p. 17.)

XXXVI (331-338). The negative element denies only spatial and temporal negations. The word ananta has no significative potency in respect of non-limitation by other things. Else, we ask, is there difference or not of ananta from the limited? If there is, then even for the ananta there is limitation by the finite (vastutaḥ paricheda). Again, the atom unlimited in time is known to be limited in space; ākāśa is unlimited in both the ways, but is different from pot etc. Do we because of this consider ākāśa as ananta?

The example is ether. Ether has parts according to Dvaita Vedānta. If a thing has parts, does it not become non-eternal? To this question the Dvaitin says that having parts is not the cause of eternality or non-eternality. Īśvara has several different attributes. Their difference is explained by the help of the category of viśeṣa which effects distinction where there is no difference. Besides there is reason for believing that ether has parts because it has conjunction with objects. As for its eternality scripture warrants it. If it be said that owing to an adjunct difference is effected in ether, the Dvaitin contends that it is not so. The adjunct merely reminds us and does not create difference. Let us examine as to whether the adjunct enters into contact with the whole of ether or with certain parts of ether? If it enters into contact with the whole of ether then there would be no difference at all. If it enters into contact with a certain part of ether, there is the establishment of the parts in ether and the adjunct only reminds us of it and does not create it. Thus there is no way of avoiding the defect of the non-existence of the probandum in the example.

XLII (405-412). The Dvaitin concludes that difference is of the very nature of the substrate and as such cognition of the substrate itself gives us the cognition of difference. Hence there is not the defect of reciprocal dependence etc., because there are no two separate cognitions. No doubt the cognition of the thing as different involves knowledge of all counter-correlates; but this in a general way is supplied by the witness-consciousness. What is supplied by the witness is an integral part of our present cognition, as may be shown by our apprehension of time, for which the witness-consciousness is responsibe. S'rī Madhva is of opinion that Time and Space are pre-conditions of all cognitions. These two elements are not cognised by perception or inference but by the witness-consciousness. The witness is the svarūpa of the soul itself.

XLIII (413-426). Time is not perceptible by the senses; the eye cannot see the colourless; the skin cannot feel the touchless; the mind cannot cognise the external; it is manifest even to the deaf from birth; hence it is cognised but not by the senses.

XLIV (427-437). The view that cognition and validity are both inferred in Bhatta's school. This is refuted after the Prābhākara view, set out earlier.

XLV (438-456). Validity is intrinsic to cognition and together with the congnition validity is manifested by witness-consciousness. Witness-consciousness cognises the validity in a cognition only when there is no defect. Defect in the cognition is the cause of invalidity. The invalidity in cognition is known by inference. The witness-consciousness does not cognise it. In such a place the cognition aspect alone is cognised by witness-consciousness. Wherever the sākṣin cognises validity there is this necessity *i.e.*, the prior establishment of the non-existence of defect. The sākṣin cognises the validity of a cognition only after the establishment of the non-existence of defect. This establishment must be effected through other tests such as agreement with other cognitions, non-existence of disagreement etc. The text is not very clear here and the commentators are at variance. Presumably what is need is coherence with other similar cognitions, non-coherence with dissimilar cognitions, non-existence of non-coherence with similar cognitions, and non-existence of coherence with dissimilar cognitions. What is the dissimilar (vijātiya)? According to one commentator it is non-existence of practical efficiency suitable to the cognition, the non-existence of that saṁvāda (vijātiyasaṁvādābhāva) is required for validity. Another commentator would require vijātiyasaṁvāda, not its absence; according to him "this is water" is the primary cognition. While another of the same form is sajātiya and the inference "this water-cognition is valid because of practical efficiency" is vijātiya; coherence with the latter too is needed.

The existence of a defect is the obstruction for the sākṣin. The removal of obstruction is through examination. The function of the examination is the romoval of obstruction. Dependence on the examination cannot be treated as a cause. The need for the removal of the examination is only to the extent of the removal of the defect. What is cognised by sākṣin is indubitable. Sākṣin does not depend on any other cognition. Its knowledge is of a self-certifying type. Hence the defect of infinite regress cannot be urged.

The dependence on examination for the establishment of the non-existence of defect does not make validity extrinsic, because examination is not a cause for the cognition of validity. Such a position would amount to this that the cause of the power of the elephant to walk is the removal of the thorn in its leg. We too well know that the elephant's power to walk is not dependent on any external factor. The removal of the thorn is the removal of obstruction.

If it be urged that invalidity too is intrinsic, it is not so, says the Dvaitin. Nowhere is invalidity cognised without the dependence on examination, whereas only in some places in respect of the establishment of validity is there dependence on examination. In respect of invalidity it is absolutely necessary ; hence it is the cause there. If it be urged that removal of obstruction is also a type of cause, then the potency of the vetra seed in respect of its giving rise to its own sprout has to be attributed to the non-existence of the forest fire. Once the forest fire burns these seeds, they give rise to a stem, not a cane. It is absurd to claim that the generation of cane has for cause non-existence of fire (itself a cause of the generation of plantain). Besides there would be the non-existence of general laws and exceptions. "Injure no living being," is the rule ; "Kill the agniṣomiya animal" is the exception ; such a relationship would have no special claim to recognition, if in every case the consequent fails merely because of a deficiency in the causal complex. We do not treat the production of an effect, say pot, when all contributory factors are present, as an instance of a general rule, and the absence of the effect when a factor is absent as an exception.

XLVIII (463-470). The witness-consciousness cognises the substrate and the counter-correlate simultaneously. The defect adduced by the Advaitin as against the concept of difference is that difference, being a relation, pre-supposes the knowledge of the substrate and the counter-correlate. Such a position puts an end to the defect of reciprocal dependence.

The simultaneous cognition of the substrate and the counter-correlate rules out the defect. Difference according to S'ri Madhva is of the very nature of the substrate itself. As aginst such a position it is urged that the substrate and the attribute *i.e.*, of difference have different characteristics. The substrate is non-dependent and the attribute is dependent, the substrate is an object of perception and the attribute is not so. The attribute is said to inhere in the substrate. The attribute and the substrate are not referred to by synonymous terms. These facts militate against the treatment of difference as the very nature of the substrate.

As against such an argument the Dvaitin points out that these difficulties are not of any consequence, because such difficulties are present in the Advaitin's concept of identity also. The concept of identity has also the abovementioned difficulties, adduced with reference to difference. Thus though jīva and Brahman as Caitanya are non-dependent, identity which is not other than jīva and Brahman is dependent on them. Caitanya is self-luminous, but not identity. Caitanya is not manifest as related to anything else; but identity is manifest as relating to Caitanya. "Identity" and "Brahman" hence have the same denotation, but they are non-synonymous terms.

If it be said that the reference to identity is a verbal one, what is it that is denied? Is Brahman denied, or is identity denied, or the relation denied, or is empirical usage denied, or the cause of empirical usage denied?

The denial of Brahman leads to the non-existence of the substrate. Without the substrate the concept of non-difference is unintelligible. If identity is denied difference becomes reality. A thing cannot be different as well as identical at the same time. If it be urged that such a thing is possible then let a thing be real as well as unreal.

If the empirical usage is to be denied, it presupposes the denial of the object indicated by the term. If the denial is of the cause, it cannot be so. The cognition of the effect helps us to assume the cause.

XLIX (471-477). In respect of the object where there is no difference still we can distinguish the non-different aspects in it. That function is attributed by Madhva to the category of viśeṣa. It is a very important category in Dvaita metaphysics. To distinguish those attributes that are not non-different from their respective substrates is the function of vis'eṣa. They are infinite in number unlike the category of vis'eṣa in Nyāya metaphysics which is found only in eternal substances. The vis'eṣas are self-differentiating (svotovyāvartaka). It is the dharma of padārthas.

Jayatīrtha argues that if the category of vis'eṣa be not admitted the scheme of relations will lead to infinite regress. At some stage at least the relation must be said to be self-explanatory. Those who accept inherence point out that inherence is not dependent on any other relation to explain itself. Instead of attributing a number of duties to relation, it is better to assume this category vis'eṣa which is only a potency of a padārtha.

Further, scriptural statements like "Brahman is knowledge, bliss" etc., can be interpreted soundly only when we assume vis'eṣa along with abheda. The attributes "knowledge" and "bliss" are not different from their substrate, Brahman. Yet they are not non-different, since the terms are non-synonymous and there is also the contingence of a host of undesirable conclusions, such as the futility of one of the terms, the leaving over of knowledge or bliss alone by the elimination of other, knowledge not being like bliss the object of unconditional desire and so on. To avoid this we have to admit non-difference, but with a vis'eṣa. (For the Advaitins refutation of the category of vis'eṣa refer to *Advaita siddhi*, p. 570.)

L (478-486). The Dvaitin's inference to establish difference is as follows. "The bodies in dispute have souls corresponding to their number, because of the attribute of being bodies." As against this inference it was pointed out by the Advaitin that the probans is inconstant in respect of dead bodies and bodies that are to be born. Though the probans is there the probandum "having a soul" is not there. Hence the inconstancy. In order to ward off this defect the probans is interpreted to mean "being the locus of enjoyment not involving reciprocal recollection". Such a probans is not present in dead bodies, because enjoyment in them is not possible. There is the negative instance, "the yogi's body". The yogin enjoys the fruit of his tapas through a number of bodies. In the yogin's body there is the absence of both probandum and probans.

ADDITIONAL NOTES

323. The reading in the Kumbakonam as well as the Belgaum text is *na ca*; but the sentence seems to be the *pūrvapakṣin's*. For, the next sentence is an objection to the solution suggested by the *siddhāntin* (Advaitin). The statement of the *pūrvapakṣin* should be taken to have begun with the present sentence and to end with *iti* before *maivam*. Hence the text should, it seems, be corrected into *nanu*.

383. What is not even cognised cannot be refuted. And you, who analyse the concept of difference in order to refute it, clearly cognise differences among the various senses.

387. The rejection of origination by a non-defective cause; this is the third case. A more prominent sublater is something like perception which, as not dependent on other *pramāṇas*, is the clearest of all.

389. *Sruti* in its non-dualist utterances may be imagined to be the sublater; it is not really so, since it can be explained otherwise; and only what has no other scope in this way can be the sublater.

400. The setting out of alternatives and their refutation proceed on the basis of difference; hence conflict with one's (Advaitin's) own activity; and the question like "Is difference different or non-different from the substrate" conflicts with one's own reasoning that there is no difference.

418. The natural colour of cloth is whiteness. Where it is blue and unclean, it is due to the colour of the dyeing material; in regard to the cloth that is dyed (and presents the colour inherent in the dye stuff) there is the empirical usage "The cloth is black

or blue"; of this usage the cause is the relation between the colour and the cloth, an indirect relation of inherence in that (stuff) which is in conjunction (with the cloth).

419. The relation here is not as simple as that between cloth and blueness; for though the movements are inherent in the sun, there is no direct conjunction between the sun and the things on earth; hence there is not the relation of *saṁyukta-samavāya*. The four elements, ether etc., belong to the earth and establish no contact with the sun; *Ākāśa* cannot fulfil this function since that too has a special quality, sound, and is in this respect on a par with the other elements; further, being one and indivisible, it could equally link the sun with all things without distinction. Hence some other substance has to be postulated linking the objects of this earth to the sun in which movements are inherent: hence the description of the relation as *saṁyukta-samavāya*.

420. Non-existences are not cognised with anything directly or indirectly; hence there would be no empirical usage of contemporaneity etc.; but there is.

424. This explanation follows the Advaitin's view of a single *Ākāśa*, being defined by objects and having the properties of the latter superimposed thereon. The position really acceptable to the Advaitin is the next one, where it is claimed that imperceptibility attaches only to *Aṁśin (Mahākāśa)*, not to particular localities which are parts thereof.

425. The syllogism about sound establishes the defect of counter-probans (*satpratipakṣatva*) in respect of the original syllogism. The argument by elimination is shown similarly to be unsound by the second syllogism about touch etc.

431. The alternatives are: does the absence of sublating cognition relate to the cogniser himself or to other persons? On the first, there is the possibility of sublation arising later. Another person's ignorance of sublation cannot validate my cognition. That no one is aware of a sublater term is impossible to establish in any

case. Similarly of the alternatives as to time, space etc. This is the unintelligibility of the analysis.

443. The quotation is from Madhva's *Anuvyākhyāna*, Chapter III, pada 3.

462. The cognition of the substrate involves also the cognition of the difference of the substrate from the counter-correlate; similarly the cognition of the counter correlate involves the cognition of the difference from the substrate; hence there is no reciprocal dependence.

476. *Samavāya* is defined as a relation located in the substrate and obtaining between that and qualities etc. Now the location is not another relation between *samavāya* and *samavāyin*. Rather does *samavāya* have to explain its own relation.

486. There is no inconstance in the first alternative; for there too is presented a difference between the real and the superimposed moons; the reality of this too being in dispute, it cannot legitimately be claimed as an exception to the pervasion; *vyabhicāra* cannot be set up in respect of the subject or what is on a par with it.

498. The non-intention of the specification applies both to "relation" and non-existence". No specification is intended of the relation whether it be *saṁsāra* or literal fetters, and no particular form of non-existence is intended either, whether absolute or that subsequent to destruction. Thus there is no inapplicability either to the *paramātman* or to released prisoner.

499. What is the use of taking the words "all relations"? The object of any qualification of the probans is to ward off inconstancy of the probans. Here "*abhāvādhikaraṇatva*" can itself serve as the probans, the pervasion being *kevalānvayin*, admitting of no exceptions; why qualify the probans further? The reply points to other instances of *kevalānvayin* pervasion *e.g.*, between namability and knowability, where the latter is the probans. Since there is pervasion even between contentness and namability, why specify the former with the words "in respect of knowledge"?

The truth is that such *viśeṣaṇas* are a part of the probans itself and require no independent fruit to justify their mention.

513. The quotations are from the *Bhagavadgītā*, Chapter 4, verse 5 and chapter 10, verse 4.

524. Those which enter as organs into a single organism are supposed to be thus conjoined; others are disjoined despite physical proximity, as of the child in the womb.

INDEX

[This index is prepared by Dr. C. Kunhan Raja. It is not a complete word index. It contains only important words; and their chief occurances are noted.]

अ

ऊ

ए

ऐ

औ

क

ख

ग

घ

च

ज

त

द

ध

न

प

भ

म

य

र

ल

व

श

स

ह

Treasure of Books

Under One Roof

Demand Any Rare Book at

www.facsimilepublishers.com

Demand Any Rare Book at:

www.facsimilepublishers.com

if not available, give information,
our team will search and update you.

Promote Knowledge:

If you have any rare book
which is not available at
www.facsimilepublishers.com,
offer it to other readers so that others can also be
benefitted with your cooperation.
The book will be printed with your courtesy.

Print & Publish:

If you wish to get your book printed or published,
we have the service for you.

Customization on Demand:

We offer customization of books
as per the demand of the customer.

Published by

Facsimile Publisher
Ashok Vihar, Delhi-110052 (India)
Website: www.facsimilepublishers.com

Distributed by

Gyan Books Pvt. Ltd.
5, Ansari Road, Daryaganj, New Delhi-110002 (India)
E-mail: books@gyanbooks.com, Website: www.gyanbooks.com

9 789333 174381